BEYOND

THE THIN BLUE LINE

CAREER STRATEGIES
FOR LAW ENFORCEMENT OFFICERS

COLIN WHITTINGTON

To request permission, contact Colin Whittington

colin.whittington@recruitingheroesllc.com

571-242-2899

ISBN: 979-8-218-44152-4
Library of Congress Control Number: 2024910421
Printed in the United States of America
First Edition: July 2024

Published by Recruiting Heroes LLC
Ashburn, Virginia
WhittingtonBooks.com

DEDICATION

This book is dedicated to my wife, Shelby, whose unwavering support and love have been my guiding light through every chapter of my adult life. To my family, whose belief in me has fueled my determination to pursue my dreams.

To all law enforcement officers who bravely step into the heart of their communities, safeguarding our way of life with courage and dedication.

Finally, to the police officers, deputy sheriffs, correctional officers, and federal agents who have lost their lives while upholding justice and protecting the innocent.

This book is for you.

CONTENTS

CHAPTER ONE
THE THIN BLUE LINE

I have stood on the Thin Blue Line. The brotherhood and sisterhood of law enforcement officers transcend time and space. A current deputy sheriff in Virginia and a retired police officer from Colorado can meet for the first time and instantly feel the bond shared by all those who have worn a badge and served their respective communities. It is a bond formed by our experiences, the things we have seen, and the ones we have lost.

The Thin Blue Line symbolizes the delicate balance and narrow yet pivotal division between order and chaos in society that law enforcement officers are responsible for maintaining. The term comes from the blue uniform police officers traditionally wear. This phrase has come to represent the close-knit community among police officers, deputy sheriffs, correctional officers, federal agents, all those who serve in this profession, and those who support our men and women in uniform.

Law enforcement, in some form or another, has been a part of our country since our Founding Fathers. Men and women have put on a uniform and gone out into their communities to serve and protect their fellow citizens. They have worked long hours and missed birthdays, holidays, and other special events. They've historically been underpaid and have faced significant criticism, hatred, and violence. In most years, more law enforcement officers are killed in the line of duty than active-duty deaths of members of the United States Armed Forces.

Despite all the challenges of being a member of the Thin Blue Line, brave women and men from all walks of life have decided to pursue this incredible profession. In 2024, the total number of law enforcement officers in America will be nearing one million. Because of this growth, law enforcement funding continues to increase, with many agencies having yearly budgets of hundreds of millions, even billions of dollars. This increase in staffing and resources will likely persist as domestic and international threats ensure we will always need these brave heroes to hold the Thin Blue Line.

Over the years, the job of a law enforcement officer has evolved from simply fighting crime. Officers are expected to play marriage counselor while on domestic assault calls, therapists while speaking with someone suffering a mental health crisis, doctors while treating a gunshot victim, and so much more. An officer can be required to respond to a motor vehicle crash, robbery, domestic assault, and homicide within a single shift and then wake up and do it all over again the next day. The expectations we set for our men and women in uniform have never been greater than they are today.

Despite the ever-growing list of duties that our officers are required to perform, the anti-law enforcement narrative in America is at its highest level in recent memory. A single officer's actions can bring nationwide feelings of hatred toward the entire profession. A split-second decision of a deputy will be replayed, examined, and dissected for weeks following a significant incident. Monday morning quarterbacking is common in this profession, with members of the community who have no law enforcement experience criticizing the actions of those whose lifelong dream it has been to serve and protect. The news media exacerbates this narrative with misleading headlines, disseminating inaccurate or incomplete information, and biased reporting, solely concerned with their pursuit of higher viewership ratings.

Between regular attrition, retirements, and staggering resignation numbers, the law enforcement profession is losing officers faster than ever. Thousands of officers a year are deciding to leave the Thin Blue Line and pursue other careers. The reasons for this exodus include burnout, financial hardships, and the current narrative surrounding law enforcement. Many more officers dream of being able to "hang it up" but feel stuck in the only career they've ever known. How can someone who has pushed a cruiser for ten or more years translate her skills and expertise in a way that a civilian employer can understand? What financial considerations must be considered when leaving a relatively stable government job? What does life look like after the Thin Blue Line?

My journey on the Thin Blue Line started on June 5, 2015. I was hired as a Patrol Deputy by the Loudoun County Sheriff's Office, Virginia's largest, full-service Sheriff's Office. After dreaming of having a career of excitement and meaning for most of my life, I was ready to take my Oath of Office. I will never forget my pride and excitement for joining this noble profession. I had the full support and love of my family. My wife even pointed out the irony of me taking my Oath of Office on National Donut Day. How lucky am I to have a wife who can find humor in a serious moment?

In my short seven-year law enforcement career, I was honored to serve alongside some of the most dedicated, passionate, and caring law enforcement officers. I experienced many highs, including being named the 2019 Virginia Deputy Sheriff of the Year, receiving two Life Saving Awards, and being promoted to Sergeant. I worked on Patrol, Community Policing, as the agency's Public Information Officer and, finally, as the Sergeant of the agency's Employment Services Section, which handled the department's recruiting and background investigations efforts. I am proud of how much I accomplished in just seven years.

During my career, I also experienced several lows, many of which are typical for officers in this line of work. I saw the dark side of humanity on many calls for service, from vicious murders to abusive spouses to neglected children. I saw a young woman who had been brutally stabbed over twenty times and stuffed in a trash can. I was the first deputy on the scene of numerous gruesome and tragic suicides. I stood in the freezing cold and rain for hours, holding the perimeter of a crime scene or while working on a crash. My best friend was struck by a vehicle as he was responding to an incident on his motor; three of my colleagues were shot by suspects while attempting to make arrests. One died by suicide. Speak to any officer in America, and they will have their own stories to share about the dark side of serving in this profession.

As I approached my seventh anniversary of joining the Thin Blue Line, I began having feelings of doubt about whether I wanted to continue in this profession. I do not recall a specific moment when I realized that I wanted something else for my life. It wasn't a particular call for service, a holiday missed, a friend who was hurt, or the media bashing my profession. It was a little bit of all of that and more. Deep inside, I knew I could no longer give my all to this profession. I was ready for my next adventure. On September 8, 2022, I put on my gun and badge for the last time. After 2,652 days, my time on the Thin Blue Line had come to an end.

As I went through my career transition, I quickly realized how limited the resources are for law enforcement officers looking to start a new career beyond the Thin Blue Line. Most police departments and sheriff's offices work hard to attract and retain their officers and deputies. However, few departments are proactive in their efforts to help their officers prepare for life after law enforcement. While many military members go through the military's Transition Assistance Program (TAP) to prepare for life after the military, most law enforcement agencies have no such program. Officers are typically left entirely on their own to navigate the transition to civilian life and the private sector.

In the years since leaving law enforcement, I've spoken with hundreds of officers, deputies, and agents who are thinking about moving to the private sector. Many people feel lost and unsure of where to begin. Some of these officers joined their respective agencies at a young age and had never worked a "normal" job before. Many have never written a resume, used LinkedIn, navigated a company's interview process, or made professional connections with civilian employers. Where can officers, deputies, and federal agents turn to for advice? This question inspired me to pursue a new purpose: help law enforcement officers transition to life beyond the badge.

This book is a guide crafted to help officers contemplate and prepare for a life and career outside of law enforcement, whether after only a few years in the profession or after 25 years of service. I'll share stories of my transition, the mistakes I made, the hardships I faced, my success, and the lessons I've learned. You'll discover how to craft a resume showcasing your skills and communicating them in terms civilian employers can understand. You will read about the power of an optimized LinkedIn profile and how networking is the real game changer in your career transition. I'll provide a roadmap for your final six months in uniform, helping you confidently prepare to step into civilian life, knowing that you have a fantastic job lined up. You'll benefit from the wisdom of other former police officers and deputy sheriffs across America as they share their transition stories and offer invaluable advice as you prepare to leave the profession.

This book will also be helpful to those who have no plans of leaving law enforcement anytime soon but know that they will want to pursue another career in the future. I have found that it is never too early to plan for life after the Thin Blue Line. If done correctly, there are steps you can take throughout your law enforcement career that can set you up for real and sustainable success in the private sector. This book encourages you to envision and plan for your life once you have hung up your uniform and gun belt for the last time. It may inspire you to consider pursuing a specialty position such as Detective, Financial Crimes Investigator, Crash Investigator, Public Information Officer, or other specialty role that can easily translate to lucrative and rewarding careers in the private sector. It may motivate you to sign up for that class you've been meaning to take or complete that certification you have always wanted. It may also encourage you to grow your professional network, which will be incredibly helpful during future career transitions. Finally, this book's resume writing and interview tips will aid you as you apply for specialty positions or promotional opportunities within your agency.

While reading this book, you will learn how to analyze civilian job postings in your desired industry. I will teach you to extract critical information, such as the required degrees, certifications, and skills companies seek. This will allow you to map out your remaining time in law enforcement and the professional development you want to accomplish before you prepare for your career transition. Not only will this make you a more valuable member of your agency, but it will also set you up to be a highly competitive candidate for your dream job in the private sector.

Reflecting on my journey along the Thin Blue Line and the experiences that have shaped my career, I am reminded of the profound bond officers share across generations and regions. The challenges we face, the sacrifices we make, and the victories we achieve collectively shape the essence of our profession and our time in law enforcement. Yet, amidst the trials and triumphs, there comes a time when we must contemplate our time beyond the badge, the gun, and the uniform.

Many officers, including myself, take the decision to leave the Thin Blue Line very seriously. It's a decision fraught with challenges, fears, uncertainties, and doubts. It is a journey filled with moments of introspection in which we reflect on our accomplishments and confront our future desires and aspirations. Nonetheless, it is a journey full of hope and possibility, an opportunity to embark on a new adventure and discover your untapped potential. You have served your community honorably and bravely. You have earned the right to think about what you want next in your life. I hope every law enforcement officer can approach this pivotal moment in their career with pride for what they've accomplished, excitement for the future, and the knowledge and skills to have a successful life in the civilian world.

Whether you are contemplating a change after a few years in the force or nearing the end of a distinguished career, I invite you to join me on this journey of self-discovery and reinvention. Together, let us embrace the possibilities ahead as we embark on a new chapter beyond the Thin Blue Line.

CHAPTER TWO
LEAVING LAW ENFORCEMENT

W hen I first contemplated leaving the law enforcement profession, I immediately realized what a massive decision it would be and the incredible impact it would have on my life. This would not be me simply leaving a "normal" 9-5 job. It was going to be a profound shift in my identity and lifestyle. For many law enforcement officers, their profession isn't just a job. It's a fundamental part of who they are. Being a "cop" was a major part of what made me. This career shaped my identity and values and gave me a sense of purpose for over seven years. Stepping away from the Thin Blue Line would mean leaving behind not only a career but a tight-knit community, a culture, and a way of life.

As I grappled with the decision to leave law enforcement, I was caught in a whirlwind of conflicting emotions and uncertainties. The thought of stepping away from this career filled me with a sense of loss and apprehension. I was quickly overwhelmed by the enormity of this decision, and I put it off for several months. These were not productive months filled with reflection and research for what I should do next. They were months of denial where I attempted to ignore the fact that I wanted to leave the law enforcement profession and start a new life and a new career.

The truth, however, soon became undeniable. I yearned for a change, something different, and a life outside the badge. I had experienced many of the negative things so often associated with the law enforcement profession. I had grown tired of the long hours, the stress, the ever-growing workload, the feeling of being underpaid, and the governmental bureaucracy, which prevented even some of the best ideas from coming to fruition. I couldn't shake the feeling that I was meant for something different.

As I began to reflect on my decision, I started to understand the importance of considering many factors before moving away from law enforcement. I knew I couldn't base such a monumental decision solely on emotion or impulse. To make one of the most significant decisions of my life, I needed to approach it with a clear mind and a strategic plan. I was well into a career that would provide relative financial and employment stability. I had already been promoted to Sergeant and had tested well on the Lieutenant's process, with another potential promotion in sight. I had accomplished many things in my seven-year career and was likely to continue to succeed if I were to stay. To make a rash decision would have been a disservice to the years of hard work and sacrifice that my family and I had made.

Some of you have completed your careers and are preparing to retire from law enforcement. Meanwhile, others are in similar positions to mine and are considering leaving the profession early. Both situations bring with them waves of emotion. Please know I am not, nor would I ever, try to talk someone into leaving law enforcement. This is a deeply personal decision and one only you can truly make. We need brave women and men to continue holding the Thin Blue Line, and I am so thankful to those who have chosen to dedicate a significant part of their lives to protecting our freedom. I would be overjoyed if, after reading this book, you decided to stay in law enforcement and continue your career in this amazing profession. However, I want to provide insight, guidance, and advice to those who have served and are now looking for the next chapter of their lives.

First and foremost, consider your well-being. The demands of this career can take a severe toll on your mental, physical, and emotional health. It can put significant strains on relationships, as can be seen by the high divorce rate among law enforcement officers. Ask yourself, and be completely honest: are you happy in this career? Would life outside the badge bring you enough fulfillment, or would you miss the rush of running code to a call, arresting a violent subject, or having morning coffee with the squad? Some officers have had enough excitement to last a lifetime and are ready for something completely different. Others love life on the Thin Blue Line and can't imagine leaving this profession. And many fall somewhere in the middle. They enjoy the mission behind the work and the feeling they get when they can help others. But they are also curious about life after the badge. Where do you fall on this spectrum? Are you ready for something new, or are there more things you hope to achieve in your law enforcement career?

Next, consider the impact on your family and loved ones. Law enforcement is not just a job; it's a lifestyle that affects everyone in your inner circle. Leaving this profession will impact your life and those of your spouse, children, parents, and close friends. Consider how they might feel about your decision and how it could change your relationship's dynamic. Do they support your decision to leave, or do they have concerns? Perhaps they are even the ones who are pushing you to look for another career. Have open and honest conversations with them to ensure that everyone's needs and feelings are being considered, especially your own.

Financial considerations are also important when considering leaving law enforcement. Evaluate your current financial situation carefully to see if your savings and alternative income streams can get you and your family through the transition period. Consider important factors such as retirement benefits, health insurance, outstanding debts, and financial obligations. Establishing an economic strategy is critical for ensuring stability as you transition into civilian life. If you are close to obtaining a full pension, examine the advantages of staying a few more years versus leaving immediately. Do you have a job opportunity lined up that will allow you to maintain or improve your current standard of living?

While law enforcement salaries may not be extravagant, the risk of facing a layoff, which is commonplace in the private sector, is minimal in the law enforcement profession, barring severe misconduct. Are you prepared to enter the civilian workforce and possibly face significant employment instability? Are you disciplined enough to save and invest for your retirement, knowing that pensions are incredibly rare in the private sector and you must be self-motivated to plan for your golden years? Evaluating the financial aspects carefully before leaving law enforcement is imperative.

Another important aspect is your skillset and how it translates to the civilian workforce. Law enforcement officers possess many valuable skills, such as problem-solving, conflict resolution, leadership, communication, and attention to detail. Take inventory of your skills and experiences and identify how they can be applied to different career paths outside law enforcement. Consider pursuing additional education or certifications to enhance your marketability in your desired field. It is never too early to start considering your next career and the steps you can take to prepare for it. Additionally, think about your long-term career goals and personal aspirations. What do you envision for your future beyond the Thin Blue Line? Are there specific industries or professions that align with your interests and values? Take the time to explore different career options and conduct research to determine which path is the best fit for you. Set realistic goals and develop a plan to achieve them, whether it involves further education, networking, or gaining relevant experience. We will go into greater detail on this topic in Chapter 3.

During your transition from law enforcement to civilian life, you will undoubtedly experience numerous challenges and obstacles. Leaving this profession can be a daunting and overwhelming experience, especially for those who have only ever known this career. There will be times of uncertainty, and you will be thrust into unfamiliar territory. However, law enforcement officers have been trained to deal with the unexpected and the unknown. Remember your training and experience. You have handled long hours, complicated crime scenes, and many other stressful situations. View your transition to the private sector as another challenge you will face and overcome. Surround yourself with your support system of friends, family, and mentors who can offer guidance and encouragement as you navigate this transition.

While you may be leaving law enforcement, remember that you will forever be a member of the Thin Blue Line and that many of your brothers and sisters in blue will always be willing to assist you. Throughout this book, I will share information about resources available to law enforcement officers looking to transition to the private sector and civilian life. Many of these are former officers or deputies who made successful transitions and are now doing fantastic work in the private sector to help other law enforcement officers do the same.

Looking back on my transition out of law enforcement nearly two years later, there are things I would do again and things I would certainly change. I invite you to draw from my successes and learn from my missteps to facilitate a smoother transition for yourself. While each transition to the private sector carries unique challenges, you will find many shared experiences. In addition to reading this book, I encourage you to connect with other former law enforcement officers who have successfully transitioned to new careers. They will undoubtedly offer their insights and perspectives, share what strategies proved effective to them, and highlight mistakes to avoid. I believe we can learn much from seeing the successes and failures of others. In Chapter 7, I will share stories of several former police officers and deputy sheriffs who successfully transitioned to the private sector and civilian life. In the upcoming section, I will share a few areas that worked and did not work for me as I switched to civilian life.

Support System

As I mentioned in Chapter 1 (remember the donut comment?), I am blessed to have a supportive wife and a caring, extended family. They believed in my decision to enter the law enforcement profession, showed incredible patience and understanding when I missed holidays and other special events, and always allowed me to speak openly with them about things going on at work. I placed great importance on keeping an open dialogue with my family and friends as I considered leaving law enforcement. I sought and gladly accepted their input on my decision to pursue a new career. This allowed me to see things from different perspectives, not just from my own narrow view.

I strongly encourage anyone considering leaving law enforcement to establish a robust support system of family, friends, and mentors. This is especially true if you choose to leave law enforcement early like me. I made many mistakes during my transition out of law enforcement, but excluding my family from the decision was not one of them. My wife and I had numerous talks over several months and came to the decision together. Seek the advice and counsel of your family and friends. It is too monumental of a decision to make on your own. When it comes time to leave your agency, you will undoubtedly feel misgivings regarding your decision. A strong support system will help you feel confident about your decision and ensure you make the right choice for you and your family.

Your support system will also be helpful as you deal with the emotional aspects of leaving this profession. As law enforcement officers, so much of our identity revolves around our job as police officers, deputy sheriffs, correctional officers, or federal agents. We form strong bonds with our colleagues and the broader law enforcement community. Transitioning away from a career deeply intertwined with one's identity can evoke a range of complex emotions, including grief, uncertainty, and even a sense of identity crisis. You will almost certainly miss the adrenaline of responding to an emergency call for service, knowing what is going on in your community, and the comradery of this profession.

The impact of my decision to leave the Thin Blue Line didn't fully hit me until over a month after my final shift. As I was getting dressed for my corporate job, just like I had done every day for the prior few weeks, I instinctively reached over to the hook that had previously held my gun belt. I had not done that once since starting my new career; however, that morning, I was tired and was running on autopilot. My muscle memory remembered the years and years of me putting on my gun belt as I prepared for my shifts.

It was at this moment that I fully realized that I was no longer a cop and would never put on a gun belt again for the rest of my life. A wave of emotions hit me as I, for the first time, fully comprehended my new reality. It was a heavy day, filled with introspection and a feeling of loss. You will most likely have your own gun belt type of day. Your support system will help you get through those challenging times.

Networking

Professional networking has been pivotal in my career trajectory, from securing my first post-law enforcement job to fueling my subsequent entrepreneurial ventures. During the final two and a half years of my law enforcement career, I served in my agency's recruiting and hiring unit. This role helped me expand my professional network within and beyond the law enforcement community. During this time, I fully recognized LinkedIn's influential role and the impact it could have on talent acquisition for my agency and my own personal branding and networking.

As the unit's supervisor, I created and managed the Loudoun County Sheriff's Office's LinkedIn page. By the time I left the agency, we had amassed the largest following of any law enforcement agency's LinkedIn page in Virginia. This platform proved incredibly helpful in attracting hundreds, if not thousands, of prospective candidates to our agency. If your agency has yet to leverage LinkedIn in its recruiting efforts, I strongly recommend you speak with your command staff about establishing an official page. Doing so will enhance your department's recruiting efforts and prove invaluable in expanding your personal and professional network.

As I ran my agency's LinkedIn page, my own network on the platform also grew substantially. I utilized my profile to highlight job openings within my agency, answer candidate questions, speak on various law enforcement topics, and discuss general recruiting and hiring initiatives. I made a conscious effort to interact with fellow law enforcement professionals and private sector leaders at conferences, training, and recruitment events. I would subsequently connect with them on LinkedIn, maintaining these relationships beyond the initial encounters. As I entertained the idea of transition from law enforcement, these connections became instrumental in exploring opportunities in the private sector, ultimately leading me to discover the company and job I eventually joined.

If you are contemplating a career shift beyond the Thin Blue Line, I strongly encourage you to explore the potential of LinkedIn and prioritize professional networking. While many law enforcement officers harbor reservations about social media, LinkedIn stands apart from platforms like Facebook, Instagram, TikTok, and X. It serves as a professional networking hub, allowing you to connect with executives, decision-makers, hiring managers, and influential individuals across various industries. Personal connections can be a game-changer in this fiercely competitive job market. We will discuss more about optimizing and utilizing LinkedIn and the power of networking in Chapter 5.

Financial Considerations

I have always been fascinated by the topics of personal finances and investments. Being financially independent has been a dream of mine for many years. While I have no intentions of retiring anytime soon, the idea of not relying on a company or the government for income for the rest of my life has long appealed to me. Much of this interest stems from my upbringing. My parents taught me the importance of saving and investing from a young age, and it has stuck with me throughout my adult life. While I am certainly no financial expert, and this is not a financial book, I do want to share some general advice and tell you some of the things I did well and not so well in this area during my transition.

The financial portion of your decision to leave law enforcement should extend beyond a simple comparison of salaries. I'll be honest. When I was first offered the job as a recruiter for an information technology firm in northern Virginia, my eyes immediately jumped to the salary significantly higher than what I was making at the Sheriff's Office. I couldn't sign the contract fast enough. However, I quickly realized there was much more to consider than salary alone.

Losing out on a government pension, government-provided healthcare, a take-home cruiser, and a significant amount of personal and sick leave are things to consider when leaving your department. While law enforcement pension amounts have been chipped away for many years now, the benefit of a pension should not be understated. Many officers who make it to retirement age will receive $50,000 - $100,000 a year for the rest of their lives. That equates to having an investment portfolio of $1 million to $2.5 million when utilizing the 4% withdrawal rule generally recommended by financial experts. Officers who make it to full retirement have a significant economic advantage and can typically make career moves based on their interests and desires and not be hamstrung by money.

This is not necessarily the case for officers leaving law enforcement early. The pension amount drops significantly for officers who leave the profession before their agency's required years of service and age. I left my agency after only seven and a half years. The pension I will receive at the age of 50 will be very minimal and far too little to support my family in retirement. Most companies in the private sector offer small 401K matches, 3-5% if you are lucky. On a $75,000 salary, that would equate to $2,250 - $3,750 a year. While not insignificant, it would take decades of saving and investing that 401K match to equal the annual amount received from a government pension. If you are only a few years from retiring, is it in your best financial interest to leave and miss out on your full retirement benefits? If you leave law enforcement early, are you disciplined enough to save for your retirement, knowing that a larger share of the burden will fall on your shoulders and not your employer? You will want to answer these questions before deciding to switch careers.

Imagine waking up a few weeks after leaving law enforcement, signing on to your prior agency's retirement account, and realizing, in horror, that thousands of dollars were missing. This happened to me, and it is one of my most embarrassing and humbling failures from my transition out of law enforcement. In addition to our pensions, the Loudoun County Sheriff's Office offers its employees three supplemental retirement accounts: a 401A, a 457B, and a Retirement Health Savings (RHS) account. Each account had its own specific guidelines regarding employee and employer contributions, matches, and, as I painfully learned, vesting schedules.

As I left my agency, each account had a modest amount of money that my department and I had contributed for over seven years. However, roughly a month later, I was alarmed to find my RHS account completely empty. I immediately contacted human resources to rectify what I assumed had been a big mistake. To my embarrassment, I was politely informed that employees only become fully vested in the RHS account after a decade of service. Therefore, I forfeited any funds the sheriff's office had contributed to my account since I resigned from my position before the ten-year mark.

Learn from my mistake and take the time to review your department's policies regarding vesting periods, rules about withdrawals, and other financial considerations. My feelings of horror and total embarrassment could have easily been avoided had I read through my department's manuals on these accounts or talked to the human resources and finance departments before leaving.

Healthcare is another essential factor to consider before switching to the private sector. Government benefits often serve as a compelling incentive for those dedicated to public service. Leaving law enforcement means leaving behind a healthcare plan that is typically superior and more cost-effective than corporate offerings. When I left my agency for a position in the IT industry, I experienced a four-fold increase in my healthcare expenses, coupled with discernibly diminishing coverage. While I did anticipate this disparity, the actual monthly cost was initially a bit of a shock. It is important to note that while each company offers its unique healthcare plan, varying in quality and price, it is crucial to factor this into your career transition decision. This is especially true for those looking to add an entire family to their plan, as the monthly premiums can become substantial.

Surprisingly, one of the things that I noticed the most when I left law enforcement was losing my take-home cruiser. Over my seven-year career, I was blessed to have been issued several awesome cruisers, including a Crown Victoria, a Dodge Charger, and a Dodge Durango. These were all fantastic cruisers in their own way. While there is much debate in the law enforcement community about what car makes the best cruiser, what mattered most to me was my agency's exceptional take-home cruiser policy. In addition to driving one's cruiser to and from work, our agency allows deputies to drive their cruisers off duty, provided they are armed and keep their radios on. This meant I hardly drove my personal vehicle during my time in law enforcement.

My wife and I bought a Ford Escape approximately four years before I left my agency. In those four years, I only amassed 20,000 miles on the car. In the year following my departure from the Thin Blue Line, I had more than doubled that mileage. This meant more wear and tear on the car and significantly more money on gas. While a take-home cruiser is probably not a compelling enough reason to stay in a career, the impact of losing this benefit took me by surprise. I still know law enforcement officers who have gone down to a single-family car, knowing they have their cruiser as a means of transportation. For them, leaving law enforcement would mean needing to buy another car or serious juggling to manage with one car between two working adults.

While I am a millennial, my mindset about coming to work has always aligned more with the baby boomer generation. Unless you are dying, you come to work. In my first five years in the profession, I only took one sick day: to take my wife to the doctor. Although I did go on several vacations, I never came close to using the amount of personal or sick leave I was given each year. By the time I left my agency, I had accrued over 1,000 hours of personal leave and sick leave. While I was paid out for my personal leave, the county's policy was that no sick leave would be paid out for employees who left before ten years of service. This meant I lost over 500 hours of leave, equivalent to three months' sick time.

Before you decide to retire or resign from your agency, familiarize yourself with your department's leave policies, especially regarding whether and how you may be paid for your accrued time. Fortunately, my agency allowed employees to "donate" leave to other employees in need. I was able to give all 500 of my hours to a fellow Deputy who had been shot in the line of duty. Hopefully, your agency has a similar program.

The Opportunity

I can honestly say that by the time I started considering leaving law enforcement, I had experienced severe burnout. I was mentally and physically exhausted and was ready to move on to my next career. This burnout led me to make rushed decisions when evaluating potential job opportunities in the private sector. I ignored several red flags regarding the company I eventually joined, including a rushed hiring process, poor employee reviews, and an outdated company website. I failed to ask pertinent questions during the hiring process to address these areas of concern. While I am not someone who lives life thinking about mistakes from my past, I do hope that highlighting my missteps will convey the importance of taking your time during this monumental decision.

Ironically, my choice to join a less-than-ideal company turned out to be one of my life's most significant decisions. It helped me discover my true purpose: helping law enforcement officers, other first responders, and veterans find amazing careers after their years of service. If I had joined a fantastic organization, I may have never been inspired to start my own company or write this book. Reflecting on my journey, I recognize how fortunate I am that things unfolded as they have, considering my poor decision-making during my transition.

The decision to leave law enforcement is a deeply personal and significant choice that requires careful consideration of various factors. Before deciding, consider your well-being, family dynamics, financial situation, skillset, career goals, and potential challenges. Don't allow momentary anger, frustration, or burnout to push you into a premature decision. While you shouldn't quit any job in the heat of the moment, this is especially true for leaving the Thin Blue Line. You have worked hard to build your law enforcement career. Take the time to consider your decision and the implications that come with it before acting.

When contemplating a career transition, it is vital to closely evaluate the industry you hope to enter, with particular emphasis on the company you are considering joining. Remember, it is not solely about whether you are a good fit for the company but also if they are a good fit for you, your career aspirations, and your values. During the job interview, ask questions about the duties of the position, the company culture, their vision for this position, and why you should work for them. Talk with current and former employees of the company to gain firsthand insights into what it is like to work there. Platforms such as Glassdoor, Indeed, and Comparably offer valuable employee reviews and are excellent resources for job seekers. Finally, assess if you see long-term career growth opportunities that fit your ambitions. We will go into greater detail about job search strategies in Chapter 6.

Goodbyes

As you transition from your law enforcement career, remember to leave your agency on a positive and professional note. Don't allow grudges or personal grievances to tarnish your excellent reputation within your agency. Express gratitude to your leadership team for the opportunities provided, say goodbye to coworkers and friends, return all your gear, and fulfill all the requirements set by your agency. Be remembered for the fantastic officer you were and not for the negative actions you took on your final days.

I used the last few weeks of my time in law enforcement to thank the various supervisors I had throughout my career, reminisce on good times with coworkers, and complete all the required administrative tasks. Remember to say your goodbyes and thank the people who played a critical part in your career. Depending on the size of your agency, you may not be able to meet with everyone; however, try to spend a few minutes with the people who made a difference in your career.

When I left law enforcement, my agency did not mandate exit interviews for departing deputies. I regret not making a greater effort to seek out the opportunity to conduct a formal interview with a member of my agency's leadership team, as I now understand the importance of such interviews. There are things I wish I had said and ideas I should have suggested. However, I was caught up in the rush of my transition and did not devote the necessary time to this important process. This was another failure in my transition.

If you are offered the opportunity to sit for an exit interview, I highly recommend you take it. Information shared during these discussions can be a powerful tool in helping the department improve and grow. Approach the interview as a chance to officially thank the agency for the opportunities they granted you while also giving constructive feedback on things that can be improved. Do not use this as a complaining session but rather as a positive interaction where you may be able to provide valuable information that can improve the careers of current and future officers.

Finally, remember to take time for yourself as you transition from law enforcement. I made the mistake of rushing into my next career without any chance to reflect, recharge, or reset from the sudden and enormous change in my life. I worked my final shift for my agency on a Friday and started working my corporate job the following Monday. I was still mentally and physically exhausted and unprepared to be at my best in my new position. If possible, take a few days, even weeks, to spend time outside of the context of law enforcement. Allow yourself the time to process the significant shift in your life, spend time with family, and have some fun. By allowing yourself to decompress and rejuvenate, you can approach your next career with a renewed sense of purpose and the energy to perform exceptionally.

The decision to leave the Thin Blue Line is undoubtedly life-changing, encompassing more than just a job title and profession change. It marks the departure from a profoundly ingrained identity that began forming during the early days in the academy. You will now be heading for new adventures and a new way of life. Remember to remain true to yourself, your values, and your aspirations. Take your time, accept the opinions of trusted friends and family members, and weigh the pros and cons of leaving this fantastic profession. You have gained incredible experiences and skills throughout your law enforcement career. In the chapters ahead, you will learn how to highlight those skills and utilize them to advance your career in the private sector.

CHAPTER THREE
PREPARING FOR THE TRANSITION

It's time to get to work! Whether contemplating an immediate departure from the Thin Blue Line or envisioning several more years in the profession, it is never too early to start planning for your life after law enforcement. There are steps you can take throughout your time as a police officer, deputy sheriff, correctional officer, or federal agent that can bolster your law enforcement career and prepare you for a successful transition to the private sector and civilian life when that time comes.

Since starting my employment agency, Recruiting Heroes LLC, in 2022, I've spoken with hundreds of law enforcement officers who want to retire or leave the profession early. Unfortunately, many wait until the last minute to plan for their next career. Many have never asked themselves, "What's next?" and are completely unsure of what type of job they want to pursue, let alone how to get it. Even those who begin the process early often fail to develop a structured plan to maximize their time and increase their chances of landing their dream job after years of service. This will not be the case for you.

In this chapter, we will create a plan for your transition. We will cover how you can assess your experience and skills and learn to translate them into terms a civilian audience can understand. We will explore industries that have historically been eager to hire former law enforcement officers and the steps you can take throughout your career to be a competitive candidate in those fields. Finally, I will share some of the training and certifications often required in various industries. With time on your side and knowledge of where you want to go, you can work toward making yourself a competitive candidate in the private sector.

One of the biggest misconceptions I hear from the law enforcement officers I work with is that they believe their experience, background, and skills are irrelevant or useless in the private sector. Nothing could be further from the truth. But how does conducting traffic stops, training rookie officers, writing search warrants, investigating frauds, conducting roll call training, and testifying in court translate to a career in the private sector? More than you might think! You simply need to learn how to articulate your experience.

When considering a transition to the private sector, the initial step involves reflecting on and writing down highlights of your law enforcement journey. This includes documenting your experience, educational background, training courses attended, and certifications earned. In the following chapter, we will delve into the intricacies of resume writing; however, reflecting on and documenting the distinctive skills acquired during your law enforcement career is a crucial step in your career transition. While not every skill, course, or certification may be pertinent to your future career path, compiling a comprehensive list is a valuable exercise, enabling you to revisit and appreciate the breadth of your accomplishments as an officer, deputy, or federal agent. This process will also help you unearth forgotten achievements and skills, which may prove instrumental in finding your next career.

Your areas of expertise may include things like law enforcement procedures, interview and interrogation techniques, legal knowledge, crime prevention, criminal investigations, surveillance and monitoring, leadership, crisis management, conflict resolution, critical thinking, report writing, courtroom testimony, computer skills, forensic knowledge, fraud investigations, and so on. Consider organizing your skills into specific categories, such as Leadership and Management, Communication and Interpersonal Skills, Problem-Solving and Analytical Thinking, and Technical and Operational Skills. Under each category, document the list of skills you have acquired during your time in law enforcement. This will help keep you organized and make things easier when writing your resume in Chapter 4.

As you write down your skills and areas of expertise, consider how each skill may apply in the private sector and the civilian world. Some proficiencies will be easy to translate to civilian terms, while others will be much more challenging. Remember, most recruiters and hiring managers in the private sector will have no law enforcement background. Documenting your experience and how it can effectively translate to a job in the private sector is essential.

I suggest writing these translations on a new document to keep your skills list clean and organized. For each skill, detail its application in your law enforcement career, try to write a civilian translation, and envision how it could benefit a private-sector job. Here are a few examples of skills you may have and how to document them.

Skill #1 – Communication and Interpersonal Skills

Law Enforcement Context

I regularly communicate with various individuals, from victims and witnesses to suspects and colleagues. I have honed my crisis intervention skills to speak with someone suffering from a mental health crisis. I also learned extensive interview and interrogation techniques to gather vital information from suspects and witnesses.

Civilian Translation

I excel in communicating with diverse groups of people, whether comforting someone in distress during a crisis or gathering crucial information from individuals involved in an incident. My ability to connect with others allows me to navigate challenging conversations with empathy and professionalism, ensuring that everyone feels heard and understood.

Private Sector Application

Communication is an essential skill in almost every profession. Law enforcement officers can use their communication skills in a variety of roles, particularly those that require instructing or supervising others. Human resource managers or specialists oversee employee relations, mediate conflicts, and communicate policies and procedures to fellow employees. They must often demonstrate empathy, listen, and communicate clearly with employees in order to increase employee engagement and satisfaction. Furthermore, corporate trainers are brought in to develop and present training programs on conflict resolution, crisis management, and workplace safety. Both positions require the employee to speak confidently and develop interpersonal relationships with others. A former law enforcement officer has acquired all of these skills through their years of service.

Another area where law enforcement officers can utilize their strong communication skills is in sales or business development. Sales are all about interpersonal relationships. As an officer, you had to build relationships with strangers multiple times per day. Doing it successfully on patrol meant a better outcome on your call for service. In business development, successful relationship building means more sales for your company and happier customers. I've found that former law enforcement officers often excel in sales and could become valuable members of their new company. When applying and interviewing for roles in the private sector, highlight your communication and interpersonal skills and how these areas of expertise can benefit the organization.

Skill #2 – Leadership

Law Enforcement Context

I was promoted to Sergeant and supervised two sworn deputies and six civilian staff members. I was responsible for setting the direction of the unit, assigning tasks, monitoring performance, handling disciplinary issues, and building team unity.

I was also a Field Training Officer for my agency. I handled numerous administrative functions, including performance evaluations, documenting and addressing deficiencies, and making recommendations to superiors regarding the trainee's suitability for completing the training program.

Civilian Translation

As a supervisor, I managed a team of two deputy sheriffs and six civilian staff members, overseeing their performance and fostering a positive work environment. I set clear objectives for the team, delegated responsibilities, addressed employee misconduct, and provided guidance to ensure all tasks were completed on schedule.

As a Field Training Officer (FTO), I played an important role in training and mentoring new officers in the agency. I guided them through the training program and provided feedback and additional training to support their professional development. As an FTO, I was also responsible for numerous administrative tasks, including performance evaluations, documenting areas that needed improvement, and making recommendations to my superiors regarding the trainee's progress and readiness for advancement.

Private Sector Application

Program management, operations management, and project coordination are critical areas in the private sector. While your official titles differed in your agency, you have many skillsets required to manage programs, oversee operations, and lead teams. Don't just view yourself as a police officer, Sergeant, Lieutenant, or FTO. Consider the administrative duties you were responsible for, the long-term projects you oversaw, your ability to build team unity, and how you worked toward a common goal. While yours were geared toward public safety, these leadership skills are incredibly transferable to the private sector, where you will be working to advance an organization's goals and objectives.

Though it may not be a term used in law enforcement, supervisors, Field Training Officers, and even regular patrol officers are project managers. It is all about articulating your job duties, skills, and experience. When speaking with potential employers, emphasize your leadership roles, how you managed projects, and how you improved the performance and efficiency of your agency's operations. These are key areas civilian employers want to see when hiring company managers.

Skill #3 – Problem-Solving and Analytical Thinking

Law Enforcement Context

During my time as a deputy, I was tasked with finding solutions to various long-term problems, including continued shoplifting by a suspected organized retail crime ring, narcotic distribution, and drunk-in-public incidents at a popular commercial business area, and steadily increasing vacancy numbers within my agency.

Civilian Translation

Regardless of my role during my law enforcement career, I was constantly required to solve problems and think analytically. Whether it be solving a string of retail thefts in my sector, coming up with a long-term solution to address excessive drunkenness and narcotic activity in a popular commercial area, or analyzing recruiting and retention data to help lower the agency's vacancy rate. One of the things I found most exciting about law enforcement was that no two days were the same. I was continuously facing new challenges that required unique solutions. As law enforcement officers, we are trained to "work the problem" and develop new and creative solutions. As crime is ever-evolving, law enforcement officers must constantly adjust and learn new ways to combat it. We are problem solvers and analytical thinkers to our very core.

Private Sector Application

Companies value adaptable and innovative professionals capable of swiftly navigating unfamiliar challenges. Few careers cultivate this agility and decisiveness as effectively as law enforcement. You have, probably without knowing, been preparing to be a phenomenal asset to a company or organization for your entire law enforcement career.

The ability to solve problems and think analytically transcends industries, making roles like business analyst and risk management particularly fitting for law enforcement officers. Your law enforcement background equips you with the analytical and critical thinking skills essential to succeed in these roles. Throughout your career, you have undoubtedly gathered and analyzed crime data, conducted thorough criminal investigations, and been put in positions to make quick and decisive decisions. These skills translate incredibly well into the private sector. With your experience, you will be able to assess potential threats and identify business opportunities effectively, making you an asset to companies in a variety of industries.

Skill #4 – Investigations

Law Enforcement Context

As a patrol deputy for the Loudoun County Sheriff's Office, I responded to various calls for service, including destruction of property, financial fraud, domestic assault, and more. I was responsible for investigating the incident, interviewing involved parties, making arrests when appropriate, and documenting my findings in detailed reports to ensure successful prosecution.

Civilian Translation

Criminal investigations are an integral part of being a law enforcement officer. While I was never a detective, I conducted criminal investigations nearly every shift during my time in law enforcement. From a simple destruction of property call to complex financial frauds to serious domestic assaults, law enforcement officers are trained to investigate a wide range of crimes. During a criminal investigation, I would take the initial report, collect evidence, interview witnesses, interrogate suspects, write search warrants, and obtain appropriate charges. Numerous skills are required to take a case from an initial report through a successful prosecution. The areas of expertise are amplified for law enforcement officers who become detectives and specialize in a specific type of crime. These detectives obtain certifications, gain experience, and become experts in their respective fields.

Private Sector Application

The skills and expertise gained from conducting criminal investigations in law enforcement are highly valuable in the private sector. Many industries seek professionals who can conduct thorough, objective, and detailed investigations to ensure compliance, investigate fraud, protect assets, and mitigate risks.

Companies hire corporate security managers to have them gather evidence, analyze data, and conduct investigations to identify and address security concerns. Insurance companies hire Special Investigations Unit (SIU) investigators to evaluate insurance claims and ensure their validity. Legal knowledge, interview skills, evidence gathering, and data analysis are crucial for a successful SIU investigator. As a law enforcement officer, you have all those skills.

Insurance firms have historically loved hiring former law enforcement officers for their investigative roles. Officers with specialized experience in crash and fraud investigations are particularly sought after; however, even regular patrol officers bring a lot of the knowledge and qualities these companies seek. If you are interested in an investigative position after law enforcement, consider companies in the insurance industry. Remember to highlight all the skills that went into solving a criminal case and how they can benefit these companies in investigating financial and insurance-related claims.

These are just a few examples of the skills that can translate well into the private sector. Continue working through your list of skills, documenting the law enforcement context in which you utilized those skills, translating them into more easily understandable terms for civilian employers, and describing how they apply to the private sector. While this task is time-consuming, it will open your eyes to how many of your skills are transferable to the civilian workforce.

This exercise will also be helpful when we work on optimizing your resume. Having the skills alone is insufficient; you must highlight and articulate those skills for potential employers. This is especially true when speaking with a recruiter or hiring manager who does not know what it takes to be a successful law enforcement officer. It will be our job to highlight these qualifications on your resume—more on that in Chapter 4.

After compiling a list of your skills, areas of expertise, and their application to the private sector, it is time to review your education, training, and certifications. List your collegiate education, including associate, bachelor, master's, Ph.D., and Juris Doctorate. Yes, I have met a few law enforcement officers with Ph.Ds and Juris Doctorates! Next, document the certifications you have obtained in your career. Some common ones for law enforcement officers include Crisis Intervention Team (CIT) Training, Field Training Officer Certification, Instructor Certification, First Aid/CPR, Digital Forensic Certification, and others. Finally, write down some of the significant training courses you have attended in law enforcement and any previous careers. Some significant courses law enforcement officers may have in their training background include the FBI-LEEDA courses, the FBI National Academy, Leadership in Police Organizations, Police Executive Research Forum, Advanced Roadside Impaired Driving Enforcement, Crime Scene Investigation Training, and many others.

Compiling a list of your education, training, and certifications is a critical exercise as it allows you to identify how these credentials can benefit you in the private sector and to identify additional schooling, training, or certifications you may want to take to prepare yourself for a future career.

As we discussed while reviewing your skills, law enforcement officers have a lot of areas of expertise that will interest potential employers. Many of these skills are backed by formal education and training. Throughout your career transition, you must highlight the degrees and certifications you've obtained and articulate how they can benefit your future employer. In the coming chapters, we will add them to your resume and LinkedIn profile and review how you can incorporate them into your answers during job interviews.

Now that you have documented your areas of expertise and your educational background, it is time to start one of the most intimidating parts of your career transition, considering what you want to do after your law enforcement career is over. Many police officers, deputy sheriffs, correctional officers, and federal agents who seek my assistance have no idea what they want to do with their lives after their careers. If, right about now, you are feeling lost and uncertain about your future career, know that you are in good company with other fantastic professionals who feel equally as unsure and confused about their futures as you do. While I can't decide for you, I can give you some important advice and tips on identifying your interests and discovering potential career passions you may never realize you had.

While overseeing my agency's recruiting efforts, I immediately realized that I enjoyed recruiting and had a natural aptitude and passion for it. Early on, I knew this was an area I could envision myself doing beyond law enforcement. Recognizing the alignment between my skills and passions and a potential career path in the private sector was critical in my transition. It provided clarity and direction for me as I approached a possible departure from the Thin Blue Line. I just had to identify the right opportunity to leverage these passions and skills.

Review your recently completed list of skills, education, training, and certifications to identify your interests and potential career passions. Reflect on your law enforcement career and the instances where you applied these skills or utilized your educational background. Are there particular skills or areas of expertise that resonate with you more strongly than others? Can you recall specific roles or responsibilities where you felt particularly fulfilled and passionate about your work?

Perhaps you enjoy the analytical aspect of investigating crimes and identifying patterns. You should consider a career as a business analyst or risk analyst. These roles require you to review data, identify trends, and solve problems within a corporate context to optimize business processes or assess financial risks. Maybe you have a passion for community engagement, public relations, and building trust with the citizens in your area. Many companies have public relations specialists or community outreach coordinators to enhance their brand's reputation and build customer relationships. Alternatively, your experience will be invaluable in today's digital age if you've specialized in digital forensics or cybercrime investigations. Corporations increasingly seek skilled professionals to work as cybersecurity analysts or information technology consultants to safeguard their digital assets. Your experience and passion for that area may be a perfect fit.

While a career in the private sector will undoubtedly be very different from what you have experienced in law enforcement, there is no reason you shouldn't pursue a profession that aligns with the interests and passions you have identified throughout your career. Reflecting on your time as an officer and identifying areas of interest will help narrow down the opportunities in the private sector you want to pursue and allow you to be more targeted in your job search process.

Job Boards

We will now utilize the power of various job boards and social media platforms to help you identify potential industries and job opportunities in the private sector that align with your interests and skillsets. Traditional job boards such as Indeed, LinkedIn, USAJobs, and ClearanceJobs are excellent starting places. LinkedIn, in particular, is a fantastic resource any transitioning law enforcement officer should utilize. I use it almost exclusively when searching for candidates for the open positions I'm trying to fill. We will discuss creating and optimizing your LinkedIn profile in Chapter 5. For now, we will focus on utilizing it to help identify your interests and extract critical information from job postings.

Under the LinkedIn Jobs section, you can search for open roles all around the country and the world. You can search for positions utilizing job titles, company names, and skills. The ability to search for roles by skill is particularly beneficial for those still exploring career paths they may want to pursue after law enforcement. Let's say a deputy sheriff with a passion for firearms is considering her options for work in the private sector. By entering "firearms" into the skills bar, she can discover thousands of open positions worldwide with the word "firearms" in the description. While not every role will fit her skills or interests, it gives her a fantastic starting point for exploring potential career opportunities she may never have known existed. The ability to search by skills or keywords is also available on other job boards, so be sure to explore a variety of websites during your career search.

Begin entering the various skills you identified as particularly interesting to you. You can narrow the search by putting in a specific location or keep the search broad by entering "United States" in the location bar, allowing you to see open positions around the country. During this initial search, don't focus on the salary or the specific companies that are hiring. This is all about identifying jobs that may fit your passions and areas of expertise. Start by reading through job descriptions and taking notes on the roles that interest you. What common themes are you noticing in these job advertisements? Is it a specific job title, industry, or task?

During your search, you may revise your initial assumptions about potential job titles and industries you thought would interest you. You may also discover opportunities you had not previously considered. Try to approach this practice with an open mind, as you may find job opportunities and industries that align with your interests in ways you had never anticipated.

As you identify roles and industries that fit your interests, pay particular attention to the specific requirements set by organizations. Companies usually start a job posting by giving an overview of their organization, detailing their mission, what they do, and other pertinent information. They will then give specific details about the role, including the daily duties and responsibilities, reporting structures, and other relevant information. Toward the end of the job posting, you will typically find the company's requirements for the role. These requirements specify the minimum skills, education, and experience candidates need to possess to be considered for the position. Companies use these criteria as a benchmark when reviewing the applications and resumes they receive to ensure candidates meet or exceed these requirements before moving them along in the hiring process.

As you will undoubtedly notice during your research, education and certification are still some of the most important and stringent requirements for many roles. This is not to say that a college degree is required for a successful career transition. Some of the world's brightest and most accomplished people have thrived without completing a formal education. However, I strongly advise you to familiarize yourself with the prerequisites for your target industries. This proactive approach will help you identify areas of your professional background that you need to improve in order to position yourself as a competitive candidate when it comes time to leave the law enforcement profession and seek new employment.

Having time to prepare for your future career is an incredible asset. This is why this book and this topic should be geared toward not only those actively looking to leave law enforcement but also those with several years left in their careers. Time allows you to enhance your skills and qualifications and further your education to improve your overall competitiveness for a role in your desired industry.

In the previous exercise of reviewing job openings in your desired industries, you probably saw skill, educational, and certification requirements you do not yet possess. Perhaps you are interested in entering the information technology industry and have noticed that many companies require candidates to have a CompTIA Security+ certification. Or maybe you hope to become a human resource manager and see a consistent theme of organizations requiring candidates to hold a Society for Human Resource Management (SHRM) Certification. Don't view these requirements as insurmountable obstacles; consider this information valuable insights into what it takes to be a competitive candidate in your chosen field. With months, maybe even years, left in your law enforcement careers, you can start to work toward acquiring those certifications and enhancing your suitability for these positions. By investing the time and effort now, you can significantly increase your prospect of making a swift and smooth transition to the private sector when the time comes.

Here are a few examples of job industries and some of the certifications that companies often require:

Cybersecurity

Certified Information Systems Security Professional (CISSP), Certified Ethical Hacker (CEH), CompTIA Security+, and Certified Information Security Manager (CISM)

Private Security

Certified Protection Professional (CPP) from ASIS International, Physical Security Professional (PSP) from ASIS International, and

Certified Security Consultant (CSC) from the International Association of Professional Security Consultants (IAPSC)

Corporate Security & Risk Management

Certified Protection Professional (CPP) from ASIS International, Certified Fraud Examiner (CFE) from the Association of Certified Fraud Examiners, Project Management Professional (PMP) from the Project Management Institute (PMI)

Emergency Management

Certified Emergency Manager (CEM) from the International Association of Emergency Managers (IAEM), Certified Business Continuity Professional (CBCP) from the Disaster Recovery Institute International (DRI), Certified Homeland Protection Professional (CHPP) from the National Sheriffs' Association

Investigations & Forensics

Certified Fraud Examiner (CFE) from the Association of Certified Fraud Examiners, Certified Forensic Interviewer (CFI) from the Center for Interviewer Standards and Assessments, Certified Computer Examiner (CCE) from the International Society of Forensic Computer Examiners (ISFCE)

Human Resources & Organizational Development

Professional in Human Resources (PHR) or Senior Professional in Human Resources (SPHR) from the HR Certification Institute (HRCI), SHRM Certified Professional (SHRM-CP) or SHRM Senior Certified Professional (SHRM-SCP) from the Society for Human Resource Management (SHRM), and Certified Professional in Learning and Performance (CPLP) from the Association for Talent Development (ATD)

Training & Education

Certified Training and Development Professional (CTDP) from the Institute for Performance and Learning, Certified Professional in Learning and Performance (CPLP) from the Association for Talent Development (ATD), and Certified Online Training Professional (COTP) from the International Council for Certified Online Training Professionals (ICCOTP)

Project Management

Project Management Professional (PMP) from the Project Management Institute (PMI), - Certified Associate in Project Management (CAPM) from PMI, and PRINCE2 Practitioner from AXELOS

Legal & Compliance

Certified Compliance & Ethics Professional (CCEP) from the Society of Corporate Compliance and Ethics (SCCE), Certified An- ti-Money Laundering Specialist (CAMS) from the Association of Certified Anti-Money Laundering Specialists (ACAMS), Certified Regulatory Compliance Manager (CRCM) from the American Bankers Association (ABA)

These are just some of the many different certifications you can pursue to make yourself a competitive candidate in the private sector. Many of these will also significantly help you in your law enforcement career. While obtaining a bachelor's or master's degree can be very beneficial, many certifications are vastly superior in their relevance to your future job and the cost and time it takes to obtain them. Depending on your agency's policies, they may even cover the costs of pursuing additional education. Take advantage of this benefit by registering for as many courses and different types of training as you can. Remember, the best investment you can make is an investment in yourself.

I strongly encourage you to go through the practices described in this chapter as soon as possible. Give yourself the knowledge and the tools you need to set yourself up for success in your future career. Law enforcement officers spend much time caring for and protecting others. I'm asking you to keep being the fantastic officer you are. However, I also urge you to prioritize your self-care and personal growth. Don't be so busy working hard on your job that you forget to work hard on yourself.

I have compiled a list of resources at the back of this book to aid you in your transition to the private sector. I have included links to many of the certifications listed above and many other services that can benefit you. Additional resources and services can also be found on my website, www.WhittingtonBooks.com.

CHAPTER FOUR
CRAFTING A RESUME FOR THE CIVILIAN WORLD

If you were to tell me that you have not looked at, thought about, or worked on your resume in five or more years, I would not be in the least bit surprised. This is a common answer I hear from many law enforcement officers in the early stages of their career transition to the private sector. So many of us joined our law enforcement agencies right out of school or after a career in the military. A lot of officers have never applied for a "normal" job before and have never needed to have a resume. Therefore, hearing from officers who have never written a resume is not unusual. Even among those with a resume, few know how to properly format and write one in a manner suitable for private sector job applications. Regardless of where you fall on this spectrum, this chapter will guide you in crafting an excellent resume that effectively highlights your skills and experience. You will also learn that a resume is not something you create once, never to be changed again. Your resume should consistently be updated, revised, and tailored throughout your career and as you apply for different positions.

A resume is a formal document that provides a concise yet comprehensive summary of a candidate's education, work experience, skills, and accomplishments. Just as companies need excellent marketing to attract potential customers and stand out from their competition, you need an outstanding resume to distinguish yourself from other candidates. You want your resume to pique the interest of recruiters and hiring managers in the private sector. In many ways, a resume serves as a marketing tool for job seekers to present themselves to potential employers. When crafted correctly, a resume offers the reader a snapshot of your qualifications and suitability for a position, highlighting relevant experiences, professional achievements, and credentials. The primary purpose of a resume is to grab the reviewer's attention and secure an interview by demonstrating your qualifications and showcasing the value you can bring to an organization.

I cannot stress enough how important a resume is in the modern-day job market. A well-drafted resume can make a significant difference in setting you apart from the other applicants. Your resume is typically the first thing a company will see and learn about you. It gives the recruiter or hiring manager a quick overview of your professional background and abilities. A tailored and well-written resume demonstrates a candidate's qualifications and suitability for a role. It reflects your attention to detail, writing skills, and commitment to present yourself professionally. Employers often use resumes as an initial screening tool to quickly identify candidates who meet a position's requirements and decide who is to move forward in the interview process and who is to be rejected. While a fantastic resume alone will not win you a job, a poor one can undoubtedly cause you to miss out on your dream role.

Format and Font

When creating your resume, it is important to choose a format and style that is both professional and easy to read. Recruiters are typically juggling 15-20 job openings at any given time, with each role receiving dozens, if not hundreds, of applications. As a result, a recruiter may review thousands of resumes every day. One of your first primary objectives is to make your resume visually appealing. A poorly designed resume, difficult-to-read font, or excessive charts and graphs can turn a recruiter against you before they've even had the chance to read about your qualifications. While I try to give each resume a fair and thorough review, overcoming the initial adverse reaction to a disorganized and overbearing resume is very challenging.

Another critical reason for having a well-structured and designed resume is to ensure compatibility with Applicant Tracking Systems (ATS). ATS are software applications used by employers across all industries to streamline their recruiting and hiring efforts. Recruiters input job postings into the company's respective ATS, automatically posting the job advertisement to various job boards, including LinkedIn, Indeed, Dice, Monster, and many more. Regardless of which job board the candidate uses to apply for the position, the candidate's resume and application are sent directly to the company's ATS. This allows recruiters to view all applications in one system rather than logging onto dozens of different websites. The ATS then scans, sorts, and filters the resumes based on specific keywords and criteria the recruiter sets. The system will score and rank the received resumes based on how strong of a fit they are for that job posting.

Unique and elaborate resume formats can often confuse the ATS, resulting in the candidate's resume being improperly scanned and sometimes even rejected. Job seekers need to use simple and clean resume formats that are easily readable by ATS. Avoid fancy graphics, unusual fonts, and complex layouts that could hinder the system's ability to read the content of your resume correctly.

I have seen some shockingly poor resume layouts and formats throughout my recruiting career. Some have been so visually distracting that it became difficult to focus on the actual content of the resume. Many candidates are unaware of the excellent, free resources and try to create their resumes from scratch. If you happen to be a creative person with strong computer skills, then certainly feel free to create your own resume template. For those like me who don't have a creative bone in their body, don't put yourself through the agony of trying to create your resume from nothing. Websites like Canva and Resume.com offer dozens of free resume templates for various industries. Even Microsoft Word has numerous resume template options to choose from. If you are struggling to find a professional resume format, visit www.WhittingtonBooks.com to download a free copy of my resume template for all of my candidates. In this technological age with nearly unlimited free resources, there is no reason to have a disappointing resume format.

When choosing your resume template, several key factors must be considered to ensure it effectively showcases your qualifications and stands out to potential employers. Your resume should be clean, professional, and easy to read. Recruiters typically spend 7-10 seconds looking at a resume before deciding whether to invest more time in the candidate or remove them from consideration. A poorly designed template that is hard to read is a sure way to get your resume added to the reject pile. Consider the industry you are hoping to enter when selecting your template. If you are targeting a creative profession, you have the leeway to use a more unique and stylized template. However, a traditional and conservative template would be more appropriate if you seek a corporate role.

Choose a clean and readable font for your resume. This is not the place for fancy fonts that require readers to squint to decipher the text. Use popular resume fonts like Arial, Calibri, or Times New Roman. The body text of the resume should be between size 10 and 12 to ensure readability while also conserving space to allow you to include all the critical information about your experience. Headings can be slightly larger, between sizes 14 and 16, to help differentiate sections and ensure more straightforward navigation through your resume.

Colored text can be an effective tool to make your resume more visually appealing; however, use it sparingly and stick to one color scheme. For example, I like to use light blue when writing job titles to make them stand out without overwhelming the reader. However, over 90% of your resume should be written in black font on a white background. Imagine how distracting it would be to read a resume with multiple colors and fonts. As is often the case in all aspects of life, you should never forget the KISS principle when writing a resume. Keep it simple, stupid!

Structure and Sequence

Next, ensure your resume has a clear and logical structure and sequence. Many candidates try to squeeze every detail of their multi-decade careers into their resumes, making the resume look overly wordy and complicated to navigate. While incorporating essential information is necessary, including some white space in the text is also important. This enhances the visual appeal of your resume, allows for easier reading, and lets you highlight key areas of expertise in your background.

Your resume should feature distinct sections, including your name, contact information, executive summary or objective, areas of expertise, work history, education, certifications, and honors and awards. Someone reading your resume should be able to locate each of these sections with just a glance. If a recruiter is forced to sift through each line of your resume to find an essential element of your experience, chances are they won't be bothered.

Now, let's discuss the actual content of your resume. Your name and contact information should be prominently displayed at the top and center of your resume. If you prefer to go by a different name rather than your legal name, that's entirely acceptable as long as it remains professional and appropriate. I would advise against using the nickname your drinking buddies have for you on your resume. Furthermore, refrain from including a picture of yourself. Not only could this introduce bias into the hiring process, but your resume should focus on your skills, achievements, and qualifications rather than your physical appearance.

Directly beneath your name, provide your location, contact information, and the link to your LinkedIn profile. I would refrain from putting your entire address on your resume. Not only would that take up unnecessary space, but limiting your location to just your city and state allows you to have some control over who knows your exact address. After all, do you want numerous companies and recruiters to have access to your precise home address? Ensure the phone number and email you provide are your personal ones. Please don't use an email address from your current employer. Not only is that cheesy, but it is also unprofessional and disrespectful toward your organization. Ensure that the email you use is appropriate. If you are still using the inappropriate email address from your youth, it is time to create a new, professional one. Lastly, I highly suggest adding the link to your LinkedIn account on your resume, as you will soon discover its importance in the following chapter.

Executive Summary

The section immediately following your contact information is arguably one of the most critical parts of your entire resume. This section is often called the Summary, Executive Summary, Professional Summary, or Objective section. This summary aims to provide a concise overview of who you are as a candidate, highlighting your experience, key qualifications, and career objectives. Keep this section to approximately 3-5 sentences in length. Begin by briefly introducing yourself, sharing your current role, the number of years of experience in your field, key qualifications that make you a desirable candidate, and finally, a statement about your career goals and aspirations.

To maximize the impact of your Executive Summary, use strong action verbs to articulate your achievements. Avoid overly generic phrases and cliches such as "hard-working" or "team player." Instead, let your accomplishments speak for themselves by citing specific examples of how you added value in your previous roles. Rather than saying that you are a "hard-working officer," you can say that you "consistently exceed performance targets by implementing innovative crime prevention strategies, resulting in a 25% reduction in crime rates." By presenting your experience in this manner, you provide concrete evidence of your abilities and showcase how you can drive tangible results. In the Executive Summary and throughout your entire resume, you should strive to incorporate quantifiable data to support your experience and achievements. Metrics such as arrest statistics, the number of officers supervised, time saved or deadlines exceeded, the revenue your division was responsible for, and the reduction in crime rates are all examples of data worth including. While this may require some initial research and effort, the positive impact adding this data to your resume will have on your career search will be significant.

The Executive Summary section, more so than any other, should be changed numerous times throughout your job search process. You can and should tailor this section for each job application you submit. For instance, if you are a police officer applying for a fraud investigator position with a bank and a recruiter position with an IT company, you should not submit the same resume for each position. The resume for the fraud investigator position should emphasize your experience with criminal investigations, report writing, and interrogations. In contrast, the resume for the recruiter role should highlight your communication, networking, and organizational skills. Tailor your resume to align with the job you hope to secure and the industry you intend to enter.

Areas of Expertise

Your resume's Areas of Expertise or Skills section is a concise list of 9-12 bullet points highlighting your specialized skills, knowledge, and abilities. Ideally, these skills and areas of expertise should align with the job you are applying for. Rather than complete sentences, each bullet point should be a specific skill or area of knowledge, limited to one or two words. Examples of potential skills to include are "criminal investigations," "crisis management," "courtroom testimony," "interrogations," "search warrants," and other skills that fit your background. Remember your list of skills that you compiled in Chapter 3? This section of your resume is where you can showcase the most pertinent ones to highlight your qualifications to prospective employers.

The Areas of Expertise section serves as a snapshot of your essential qualifications, allowing recruiters and hiring managers to quickly assess if you have the necessary expertise for the position. By demonstrating your specific areas of expertise, you can quickly and efficiently establish your suitability for the position and capture the attention of potential employers. Imagine a recruiter for an insurance company tasked with finding a candidate for an insurance claims investigator position. The recruiter is told to find a candidate with experience conducting criminal investigations, writing detailed reports, conducting interviews, and examining evidence. The recruiter could look at the well-written resume of a police officer and immediately see all those skills in the officer's Areas of Expertise section. Without reading further, the recruiter would recognize this candidate as a potential fit for the position. That is the power of this section.

Similarly to the Executive Summary, an effective Areas of Expertise section requires you to make minor alterations for each job application. Review the job posting and identify the key skills and qualifications the company is seeking. If you have experience with a particular skill the company is looking for, ensure it is included in your Areas of Expertise section. This is a particularly important step in the modern job market, where many companies utilize ATS. In most ATS, resumes are scored based on their alignment with the job description, including key skills and qualifications. For instance, the ATS we use at Recruiting Heroes gives each resume a percentage score based on how closely it aligns with the job description, ranking candidates from highest to lowest. While we prioritize reviewing every resume received, this is not always true with other companies. Therefore, optimizing your resume to score highly in the ATS is essential to ensure it is viewed by an actual recruiter and not just by the system. An ATS can only decide which resume best fits a position, not necessarily the best candidate. Incorporating desired skills and qualifications from the job description is crucial in advancing in the hiring process.

Professional Experience

The Professional Experience section of your resume is where you showcase your work history, detailing your employment experience, job responsibilities, and achievements. This section should be structured in reverse chronological order, starting with your current or most recent position and working backward. Create a header for each organization you have worked for. Be sure to include the location and full dates of employment with that agency or organization. Next, use a sub-header to highlight your job title, the specific unit or division to which the role was assigned, and the dates you served in that role.

Avoid using unique or made-up section headers or job titles. I have seen candidates refer to themselves as "Marketing Ninja," "Brand Storyteller," "Peacekeeper," and many other unusual titles. Remember, Applicant Tracking Systems will scan your resume to determine if you are a good fit for a position. Writing unique job descriptions that the ATS cannot recognize may harm your chances of landing your dream job.

When describing your job duties and responsibilities, use bullet points to improve the readability of your resume and to drive the reader's attention to specific key achievements. Paragraph-style descriptions are not visually appealing on a resume and may cause important aspects of your work history to be overlooked. Utilize bullet points effectively by including strong action verbs and specific, quantifiable achievements to describe your accomplishments. Avoid using vague and generic phrases when describing your job duties and achievements. You have a finite amount of space on your resume. Make every sentence count. Don't just tell the reader that you are a fantastic candidate; show them by including statements such as "Seized illegal weapons, narcotics and stolen property while executing over 30 search warrants, resulting in the arrest of ten suspects and 50 felony charges" or "managed an annual divisional budget of $1 million, optimizing resource allocation and ensuring cost-effective operations."

While it may be tempting to detail every position you have held for the past several decades, the standard for acceptable resume length is two pages. No recruiter wants to sift through a 5-10-page resume, regardless of how fantastic the candidate is.

So, what do you do if you have had a multi-decade career? Focus on the roles you have held for the past 10-15 years. List each role and give details about your qualifications and experience in those positions. Then, create a header for "Additional Experience" and list your remaining roles with only the dates of employment, omitting additional details. While it may seem counterintuitive to not highlight all your experience, employers are primarily interested in your most recent employment history rather than the work you did twenty years ago. Remember, the job of your resume is to get you to the interview phase of the hiring process. You can expand upon and add to your fantastic experience once you sit before the recruiter.

Many law enforcement officers struggle when writing resumes due to police jargon and industry-specific terms. While these terms may be acceptable when applying for specialty positions or promotions within your agency, they can confuse recruiters and hiring managers who most likely have no law enforcement background. Instead of simply stating you are an FTO, say you are a "Field Training Officer, responsible for training, mentoring, and supervising new officers to the agency." Instead of saying that you "ran code to calls," write, "responded promptly to significant incidents utilizing my police cruiser's emergency lights and sirens to ensure rapid arrival and effective response." Pretend that the person reading your resume has zero knowledge about law enforcement because, more likely than not, they won't.

Education, Certifications, & Awards

The remaining sections of your resume should include:

- Your education.
- The relevant training courses you've attended.
- The certifications you have obtained.
- Any awards or honors you have received during your career.

Each section should have its own distinct header to allow the reader to distinguish between your resume's segments easily.

In the Education section, provide a comprehensive overview of your academic background. Start with the highest level of education you have completed and work backward from there. Include the name of the institution, its location, and the degree you earned. While it's acceptable for recent graduates to include their graduation year and GPA, I generally advise candidates with extensive work experience to omit this information. This advice also applies to high school information. If you are a recent high school graduate with limited work experience and no further educational background, you can certainly include your high school diploma information on your resume. Otherwise, omitting high school information is recommended, as most employers will assume you have a high school diploma due to your law enforcement background. If you have no additional educational experience to list, you can remove the entire section, allowing you to focus more on other areas of your background.

As law enforcement officers, we attend many training classes to meet our state requirements and further our careers. A single officer may have 50 or more pages in their training records. In Chapter 3, you began documenting all the training you have attended and the certifications you have obtained. You will now want to narrow this list to only the most significant ones you want to include on your resume. Consider the industry you hope to enter and how each certificate can help you. While being certified as a Beanbag Shotgun Operator is cool, will it help get you a job as an IT Help Desk Technician? Probably not. Aim to list 5-10 of the most significant certifications and training courses you have completed. If you are actively pursuing a certification that will benefit your future career, including it on your resume with an expected completion date is acceptable. This will show recruiters and hiring managers your motivation and commitment to continuous learning in their industries.

The last section of the resume is the Honors and Awards section. You have had a fantastic law enforcement career and should be very proud. Listing any honors or awards you have received is an excellent way to highlight your professionalism and passion for your work. A Life Saving Award, Investigator of the Year Award, and Meritorious Action Award are all examples of achievements you should highlight on your resume.

Unfortunately, a lot of the excellent work by our women and men in uniform is never recognized or rewarded. Therefore, if you have not received any notable honors during your time in law enforcement, that is perfectly fine. This section is not critical but serves as a valuable addition to your resume. Furthermore, if you have difficulties keeping your resume to two pages, consider shortening or omitting this section to allocate space for other information.

Congratulations, you did it! You have now crafted a compelling resume that is both visually appealing and effectively highlights your qualifications, experience, and education. Remember to always tailor your new resume to the job you are applying for. While it may seem tempting to "throw" your resume at every job opening and see what sticks, you will most likely be wasting your time and potentially hurting your chances with certain companies. Many organizations, especially the well-established ones, maintain detailed records of applications they receive and their status. Applying for numerous jobs at a company utilizing the same resume can flag your application, significantly reducing your chances of securing a job with that organization. We will continue discussing job search strategies in Chapter 6.

Some of you have undoubtedly heard about professional resume writers and perhaps wondered if they are worth the money. The answer: it depends. There are plenty of excellent professional resume writers; however, there are just as many terrible ones. Furthermore, the price for a resume can range from just a few hundred dollars to well over a thousand. If you are considering purchasing a professional resume, ask the company for sample resumes they've written, customer reviews, and transparent pricing. If they cannot provide you with those basic requests, I'd suggest running in the other direction.

I have been writing resumes for law enforcement officers for many years. I genuinely enjoy highlighting their incredible skills and qualifications to help them find their dream jobs in the private sector. Given my experience as a deputy sheriff and a recruiter, I can effectively translate many of their specific law enforcement skills and write them in terms easy for civilian hiring managers to understand.

If you are struggling with your resume, contact us at info@recruitingheroesllc.com, mention reading this book, and I will give you 25% off any of our services. Want to save even more money? Take a picture of yourself reading this book and share it on any social media platform, and I'll give you 50% off! Not only will you receive a fantastic new resume, but you will also help me reach more law enforcement officers who can benefit from the information in this book. Furthermore, I would be honored if you would consider leaving an honest review of this book on Amazon. I'd love to hear your thoughts. Moreover, reviews will make this book more visible to other law enforcement officers.

I know I have thrown a ton of information at you in this chapter. To simplify things, here is a concise to-do and not-to-do list for your reference as you refine your resume. Use the space on the right side to jot down notes or check off completed tasks as you go through the resume writing process.

COLIN WHITTINGTON

Resume To-Do List	Your Notes
Clean, professional layout	
1-2 pages in Length	
Professional font	
Bullet point format	
Spellcheck and grammar	
Full name	
Current location	
Phone number	
Professional email address	
LinkedIn profile	
Executive summary consisting of 3-5 sentences	
9-12 most relevant skills	
Professional experience in reverse chronological order	
Your job title for each position	
Company name and location	
Dates of employment	
Key responsibilities and quantifiable achievements using action verbs	
Education with the name of the institution and degree type	
Relevant certifications and training	
Optimized and tailored resume for each job	

Resume Not-To-Do List	Your Notes
Including personal information like age or marital status	
Including hobbies, unless they directly relate to the position	
Lying about qualifications	
Cliches and generic phrases	
Excessively long resume	
Inappropriate email address	
Flashy designs, colors, or graphics	
Spelling and grammatical errors	
References – the company will ask for them if they are needed.	

CHAPTER FIVE
THE POWER OF LINKEDIN AND PROFESSIONAL NETWORKING

Law enforcement officers often approach social media with caution and skepticism, reluctant to make themselves readily visible to the public. In our time in law enforcement, we have witnessed so many terrible things and interacted with the worst parts of society that we tend to exercise restraint in this domain. To this day, I still do not have my full name listed on my Facebook account, concerned that individuals I have arrested might be able to discover personal information about my family and me. However, LinkedIn and professional networking have been instrumental in my transition to the private sector and the growth of my business. I hope the distrust of social media will not dissuade you from exploring and capitalizing on the power of LinkedIn in your job search process.

In today's digital world, LinkedIn has become an integral tool for job seekers in various industries. LinkedIn is a professional networking platform designed to connect hundreds of millions of people worldwide. Job seekers can highlight their qualifications, skills, and experience. You can create a comprehensive profile, join industry-specific groups and forums, share articles, and network with other professionals. You can also use LinkedIn to search and apply for thousands of jobs worldwide.

Developing a strong LinkedIn profile is crucial in your job search process because recruiters from all industries are searching for their ideal candidate using this platform. Many recruiters, myself included, dedicate more time to reviewing candidates' LinkedIn profiles than resumes. This platform allows candidates to share significantly more information about their qualifications, work ethic, knowledge, and skillset than they could ever incorporate into a two-page resume. A compelling LinkedIn profile will have recruiters contacting you to recruit you to their company. Ensure your profile is complete, easily accessible, and accurately represents you as a candidate, employee, and person. In this chapter, I'll guide you through setting up and optimizing your LinkedIn profile, how to use it to grow your professional network, and how to identify job opportunities in your desired industry.

Although I activated my LinkedIn profile over ten years ago, it wasn't until I became the sergeant of my agency's recruiting and background investigation unit in 2020 that I became an active member. In that position, I leveraged the platform to find candidates to join my agency for both sworn and civilian positions. I regularly posted jobs, answered questions, and quickly transformed our agency's LinkedIn page into one of our best recruiting resources.

I also used the platform to connect with law enforcement professionals and leaders of other industries worldwide, steadily growing my personal network. As I was considering leaving the Thin Blue Line, the network I had been growing on LinkedIn became incredibly valuable. It facilitated conversations with leaders in various industries, forged relationships, and allowed me to discover opportunities in the private sector. One of these conversations led to me finding a job advertisement for a recruiter position with a company in my area. A LinkedIn connection of mine introduced me to the hiring manager, and before I knew it, I had been offered the position.

Since leaving law enforcement, my LinkedIn network has only continued to grow. I utilize the platform to find candidates for our client's open positions and while working with law enforcement officers and military veterans to identify job opportunities for them. This platform's impact and potential for both employers and candidates are enormous. If you have not registered a LinkedIn profile or have not been active on the platform, make it a priority in the days and weeks ahead to dedicate time to developing your presence on LinkedIn and growing your network. This is an important step, even if you are years away from your next career. Building a strong network takes time. The more runway you give yourself, the better prepared you will be for your transition to the private sector.

Like most websites these days, LinkedIn makes the registration process incredibly easy. Visit their website and click "Join Now" at the top right corner of the page. When prompted, enter your name, email address, and desired password, read LinkedIn's terms, and click "Agree & Join." Lastly, go to your email address and open the verification email sent to you by LinkedIn. Click on the link to verify your account, and you're done. It's that easy!

Now comes the more challenging part. Completing and optimizing your LinkedIn page will take significantly more time and effort than the registration process. However, if done correctly, it will yield fantastic results in your career transition. Just as Rome wasn't built in a day, perfecting and optimizing your profile will not be done overnight. You will continuously find new areas to improve and add to. In the following sections, I will give step-by-step instructions on optimizing your LinkedIn page. I suggest you open your LinkedIn profile and work on each section as you read this chapter. Let's get started.

Profile Picture

A candidate's profile picture is the first thing recruiters and hiring managers will see when you come across their screen. Unlike other social media sites, LinkedIn is primarily for working professionals looking to network, find a new job, or find candidates to recruit. Your profile picture should reflect your professionalism. Don't think of LinkedIn as another Instagram or Facebook. Leave your pictures of your beach vacation or at the football game for other social media platforms. While you don't necessarily need a photographer to take your LinkedIn picture, you want to look professional and polished. Choose clothing appropriate for a job interview, including a tailored suit, shirt and tie, a professional top, or a dress. The background should be clean and uncluttered, preferably a plain wall or a professional setting such as an office or conference room.

Instructions:

Step 1: Save the desired image to your laptop, computer, phone, tablet, etc.

Step 2: Click on the profile picture area from your LinkedIn profile page. Select "Add Photo" and select the image from your computer files.

Step 3: Adjust the photo if needed using the zoom and straightening features on the screen. Ensure that your entire face is within the circled area.

Step 4: Click "Save Photo."

Background Photo

Each LinkedIn profile allows users to upload a background picture displayed horizontally at the top of your profile page and behind your profile picture. I highly recommend having an image in this area and not leaving it blank. Leaving this section empty makes your profile look incomplete. This image should show the viewer something about yourself. It can be a hobby, a part of the world that you love, interests, etc. Some people also utilize this section to highlight a business they own or a side hustle they run.

The dimensions for the background image are 360 pixels by 120 pixels. You can find free background images on Google by searching "LinkedIn background pictures." If you are in a creative mood, you can also use www.Canva.com to design your background image for free. On Canva, select "Create a design," in the search bar, type in "LinkedIn Background Photo." Canva will set the correct dimensions for the image. You can then begin designing your background photo. Here are the steps to upload a background photo onto your LinkedIn profile:

Instructions:

Step 1: Save the desired image to your laptop, computer, phone, tablet, etc.

Step 2: From your LinkedIn profile page, click the pencil icon in the background image area.

Step 3: Select "Change Photo" and select the image from your computer files. Adjust the photo as needed.

Step 4: Click "Apply."

Headline & Introduction Section

Your Headline and Introduction sections are some of the most important parts of your profile. Your Headline is displayed directly under your profile picture and should be used to briefly highlight your qualifications as a candidate and employee. The information you have here will show recruiters and hiring managers who you are, your background, your skills, and your desired industry. You can be creative in this section to draw viewers' attention to your profile. However, LinkedIn only allows you to write 220 characters in your Headline section, so you must be concise with your wording. Here is an example of what a Lieutenant could write as his LinkedIn Headline:

Police Officer | Lieutenant | Seeking to utilize the skills gained during a diverse law enforcement career to further an organization's operational and managerial needs.

Instructions:

Step 1: Click on the pencil icon in the upper right corner of the introduction section of your profile.

Step 2: Type in the statement you wish to have as your Headline. LinkedIn has an AI feature that can assist you should you need help.

Step 3: Click "Save."

Next, you want to ensure that the remaining areas of your Introduction and Contact Info sections are complete. I see a lot of incomplete profiles while I am searching for candidates. An unfinished profile can show a lack of effort on your part and cause recruiters to hesitate to contact you. In this section, you can input your name, location, and contact information. Some candidates are more private than others. Decide what information you are comfortable sharing. You can adjust your selection anytime, so don't feel it is set in stone.

Instructions:

Step 1: Click on "contact info."

Step 2: Click on the pencil icon.

Step 3: Complete any fields you wish to have filled. I typically suggest that candidates include at least their email address. This gives recruiters an additional way to contact you. I do not recommend adding your full address or birthdate for privacy reasons. If you wish to display a personal or company website, you can include that in the "Website" section.

Step 4: Click "Save."

Job Preference

A handy feature of LinkedIn is the ability to highlight if you are interested in learning about new roles and your desired position and industry. Once you spend time on LinkedIn, you will undoubtedly notice that some members have green "Open to Work" banners around their profile pictures. This means that the person is looking for new job opportunities. I suggest active job seekers put the "Open to Work" banner on their profile if possible. This green banner notifies recruiters that you are interested in new roles, increasing the chance that you will be contacted. But be aware. This banner is public for everyone to see, which means your coworkers, supervisors, and command staff members on LinkedIn will know that you are looking to leave your department.

A more discrete option for those looking to transition from their current job is to utilize LinkedIn's "Open to Work" feature that is only visible to users of "LinkedIn Recruiter." This is perfect for candidates who do not wish to inform their agency that they are considering leaving. LinkedIn Recruiter is a $7,000 - $10,000 a year resource used by recruiters in the private sector. Because of the high cost, it is highly unlikely that casual LinkedIn users, your coworkers, or your supervisors will have that premium service. This means you can show recruiters from the private sector that you are interested in new opportunities while not letting members of your agency know.

The Job Preference section of your LinkedIn profile also allows you to share information about your career interests. Start by adding up to five job titles that interest you. Next, share whether you are interested in working on-site, hybrid, remote, or any combination of those three. You can then share the locations where you would be willing to work. Next, you can share how quickly you are looking for a new role. LinkedIn gives you two options, "Immediately, I am actively applying" and "Flexible, I am casually looking." Finally, you can say if you are interested in full-time, part-time, contract, temporary, or internship work.

Place as many job locations as possible in the "Job Location" section. When searching for candidates in certain areas, recruiters will filter the results only to show candidates interested in working in those areas. Adding locations where you are willing to work will increase your profile's exposure. If you want a remote role, add "United States" as a location. This will make you visible to recruiters searching for candidates for their remote roles nationwide.

Instructions:

Step 1: Click the "Open To" icon in your introduction section. From the dropdown menu, click "Finding a new job."

Step 2: Under "Job Titles," list up to five job titles you are interested in.

Step 3: Under "Location Types," I highly recommend checking On-site, Hybrid, and Remote. This will show recruiters that you are open to any work setting and will not limit you to one type or another.

Step 4: Under "Job Locations," select the areas of the country in which you would be interested in working on-site. If you are open to relocating anywhere in the country, you can enter "United States." The more locations you enter, the higher the likelihood you will be contacted as recruiters search for candidates based on where they are willing to work. For the remote location, enter "United States":

Step 5: If you are actively looking for a new job, we suggest clicking "Immediately, I'm actively applying." If you are just casually looking, you can select "Flexible. I'm casually looking."

Step 6: Job Types—List any job you are interested in (Full-time, contract, part-time, internship, temporary). I typically suggest that candidates list "Full-time" in this section.

Step 7: Select the visibility setting for your Open to Work status. You can select "All LinkedIn Members," which is visible to everyone on LinkedIn and adds a green "open to work" banner to your profile picture. You can also select "Recruiters Only," which does not display the banner and only shows information to individuals who have purchased LinkedIn Recruiter.

Step 8: Click "Save."

About Section

The About section of your LinkedIn profile is an excellent place to tell readers who you are, what you have accomplished in your career, and where you hope to go. Think of it as a summary of your professional life. Start by writing a compelling first sentence that grabs the reader's attention. Then, highlight your unique skills, expertise, and career aspirations. You can enter up to 2000 characters in your About section, so utilize them effectively. Unlike a resume, it is common and acceptable for candidates to refer to themselves in the first person in this summary. While you want to maintain a professional tone, I like to keep the About section conversational to make it more relatable and engaging for potential readers. Be authentic and sincere in communicating your brand and sharing your career goals and objectives.

Instructions:

Step 1: Click the "Add Profile Section" and then click on the "About" Section.

Step 2: Type or copy and paste your About statement for your profile. Remember, it must be less than 2000 characters.

Step 3: Click "Save."

Experience

The Experience section is a crucial part of your LinkedIn profile, where you will showcase your professional journey and qualifications to potential employers. Think of this section as a digital version of your resume. In the previous chapter, we worked on creating a fantastic resume for you. We now want to integrate the information from your new resume into the Experience section of your LinkedIn profile. This includes agencies and companies you've worked for, your various job duties and responsibilities, and the skills you have gained in those roles.

It is important to be thorough when completing your work experience. Recruiters in the private sector utilize LinkedIn to "source" or look for candidates for their open roles. Instead of just waiting and hoping for competitive candidates to apply for their positions, recruiters actively look for candidates with the desired skills and experience. They do this by searching for specific keywords, areas of expertise, certifications, and other qualifications. Adding details about your experience and skill set will significantly increase your chances of recruiters contacting you and trying to recruit you to their companies.

Similarly to your resume, you want to list your current or most recent job first and go in reverse chronological order from there. Be sure to include the agency or organization you worked for, the job title, and dates of employment. You want to highlight your job duties and responsibilities in the description section. Since you now have a fantastic resume, I suggest utilizing the wording from your resume to bolster your LinkedIn profile. Using the bullet point statements from each job title on your resume and incorporating them into your LinkedIn Experience section is a fantastic way to ensure your profile is as optimized as possible.

Instructions:

Step 1: Click "Add profile section" from your LinkedIn profile.

Step 2: Click "Experience" to add this section to your resume.

Step 3: Click the "+Add position" button to add your work experience to your profile.

Begin with your most recent role first and work backward.

Step 4: Enter job details such as job title, company name, location, and dates of employment.

Step 5: Utilize the information from the corresponding role on your resume to add the description for your role on your LinkedIn profile. Be sure to quantify your achievements, highlight your successes, and mention the skills you developed in this position.

Step 6: Just as Applicant Tracking Systems screen resumes for specific keywords, recruiters will source candidates based on certain skills and areas of expertise. Each job title on LinkedIn allows you to add a list of skills you gained and utilized in performing that role. Refer back to the list of skills you documented while reading Chapter 3 of this book. Consider which skills will best highlight you as a candidate for the industry you hope to join.

Step 7: Add multimedia elements or links to your various jobs to make your profile more engaging and interesting. If you have documents, pictures, videos, or other media you want to share for that specific role, you can upload them in the job entry area.

Step 8: Click "Save."

LinkedIn is a fantastic place to highlight the skills you have gained during a diverse law enforcement career. The list of potential skills that can be added to a LinkedIn profile is endless. Skills are an excellent way to include keywords in your LinkedIn profile. Like a resume, you want to ensure that your profile highlights the correct skills for your preferred industry. Just as Applicant Tracking Systems screen resumes for specific keywords, recruiters will source candidates based on certain skills and areas of expertise.

Education

The Education section of your LinkedIn profile is where you can showcase and highlight your educational achievements. You can display your degrees, relevant classes, and projects to further demonstrate your expertise in a specific area. Similarly to previous sections, you can add an Education section to your profile by clicking "Add profile section" and selecting "Add education."

When completing this section, start by listing your highest level of education first, followed by any additional degrees you have obtained. Nearly every major college or university has its own LinkedIn page. Be sure to name and tag the school you attended in your Education section, as recruiters and hiring managers like seeing candidates from their Alma mater. Including this information on your profile can give you a leg up on other candidates and a fantastic conversation starter with potential employers.

In addition to listing your school, degree, field of study, and graduation year, this section allows you to include honors, awards, and extracurricular activities that are relevant to your professional profile. Providing all of this information highlights your academic achievements while also providing insight into your skills, interests, and dedication to lifelong learning and development.

Licenses and Certifications

As we discussed in Chapter 4, companies in the private sector often put a great emphasis on wanting candidates who have specific certifications or licenses. You have already identified and possibly started working toward the certifications and licenses most applicable to your desired industry. As you complete the courses and obtain certifications, you want to highlight them for the world to see. LinkedIn provides a section to add details about these key areas of your background.

One of the most common ways recruiters search for candidates on LinkedIn is by entering the required certifications or licenses for their specific position. LinkedIn will then show them all the candidates with these certifications listed on their profiles, allowing the recruiter to quickly see a list of eligible candidates. Having a certification does not mean much in the recruiting and hiring world unless you make it easily visible for companies to see. Be proud of your hard work by displaying your certification or license on your profile.

Click on "Add profile section," then click on "Recommended," and finally click on "Add licenses & certifications."

Honors & Awards

Your LinkedIn profile's Honors and Awards section offers a valuable space to highlight and celebrate some of your achievements, awards, and honors throughout your career. Perhaps you won a Life Saving Award, Meritorious Service Award, Instructor of the Year, or any other honor celebrating your incredible achievements. Let's add them to your LinkedIn profile. This will showcase your professionalism and passion for your work.

Click the "Add to profile" button, click "Additional," and then click "Add honors & awards." For each entry, describe the award to help others understand the significance of your achievement. You can include information about the organization that gave the award, the criteria for selection, and any specifics you can share about the actions that led to you winning the award.

Featured

The Featured section is one of my favorite parts of a LinkedIn profile. However, LinkedIn members rarely utilize it. I think of this section as a type of highlight reel of your professional life. In this section, you can include articles and newsletters you have written, links to media stories that mention you, letters of recommendation from previous supervisors, and much more. My favorite thing to include in the Featured section is your resume. You can upload your entire resume and make it a prominent part of your LinkedIn profile. This will attract the attention of recruiters and hiring managers, who can review your professional background, qualifications, and areas of expertise. I always encourage my candidates to include their resume on their LinkedIn profile.

To add the Featured section to your profile, click on "Add profile section," then click on "Recommended," and then "Add featured."

You can then begin uploading documents, articles, links, and images to your profile.

You have now completed the significant portions of your LinkedIn profile! While the sections I mentioned are your profile's most critical areas, LinkedIn allows you to add additional information, such as career breaks, volunteer experience, patents, languages, and more. I encourage you to look through all the available options by clicking the "Add to profile" button and determine which sections are most relevant to you.

While it may not be natural for everyone, especially for many law enforcement officers, I suggest being an active member on LinkedIn. By regularly updating your profile with achievements, certifications, and new skills, you will grow your network and present yourself as a proactive and determined professional. By growing your network, posting exciting content, and commenting on other people's posts, you also become more visible and increase your chances of being noticed by recruiters and hiring managers. My activity on LinkedIn was a significant factor in obtaining my first job in the private sector. I believe it can have the same positive effect on your career.

As your career progresses, you will meet and interact with various professionals at conferences, training courses, and networking events. Capitalize on these encounters by exchanging contact information and connecting with them on LinkedIn. Furthermore, utilize the "My Network" feature at the top of your LinkedIn profile to discover individuals from your organization, alumni from your school, or those with the same job titles and interests as you.

You can connect with people and grow your network by sending connection requests. Others will also send you requests. Avoid sending excessive connection requests, as LinkedIn imposes a weekly limit. Prioritize networking with individuals you have met, worked with, or share common interests with. A robust list of valuable connections is far more important than focusing on the number of connections. I'd be thrilled to connect on LinkedIn. Send me a connection request and mention reading this book!

Job Postings

LinkedIn is obviously also a fantastic resource for finding jobs. By clicking on the briefcase icon at the top of your profile, you can search for various roles worldwide. You can search by company, keyword, skill, and job titles. You can add numerous search filters, including salary, industry, on-site, hybrid, remote roles, etc. You can also set job alerts for your specific area of interest. This will allow you to receive email alerts from LinkedIn when a role with your set specifications is posted, allowing you to be amongst the very first candidates to see the position and apply. Upon entering your filters for the type of position you seek, you can turn on the job alert by clicking the "set alert" button near the top of the page, just above the job advertisements.

Job postings typically include a wealth of information about the job itself, the company, the location, the job description, and more. For jobs posted on LinkedIn, the top of the posting will always show the title of the position followed by the company's name, the location of the role, when the role was posted, and the number of applicants. Candidates often get nervous because of the high number of applicants shown on many job postings. Don't let this deter you from applying. Contrary to how it may seem, this number does not necessarily reflect the actual number of candidates who applied for the position but rather those who clicked on the application link. Many applicants browse through an application, never completing or submitting it. This means that the number of applications submitted for the position may be significantly lower than shown.

Companies have the option of listing the starting salary range for the position. While many companies are still resisting the push for pay transparency, there has been a remarkable shift toward companies being more upfront about the starting salaries for their positions. I suggest that you approach companies who are ambiguous about their salaries with caution. I recommend candidates request salary information early in the hiring process to ensure they are not wasting their time on a position that will not meet their salary requirements.

The job advertisement will then display the size of the company, its industry, and any connections you have within the company's workforce. Remember when I stressed the importance of having a comprehensive LinkedIn profile? The value of a robust LinkedIn profile and strong professional network truly shines during your job search process. You may discover a shared connection with current employees of the company you are applying to, that you attended the same college as the recruiter, or that you previously worked at the same company as the hiring manager.

In today's competitive job market, who you know is often more important than what you know. Leverage these connections by reaching out to members of your target company, inquiring about their experiences with the organization, and seeking their insights and assistance. You will be pleasantly surprised by people's willingness to help those in the job search process. A thoroughly completed LinkedIn profile will allow you to discover connections you would otherwise have overlooked and utilize them to further your career.

The job posting will also outline the skills the company deems most critical for this position. LinkedIn will show you how many listed skills are reflected on your profile. This helps you gauge your suitability for the role and guides you in tailoring your resume and LinkedIn profile to align with the desired qualifications more closely. For instance, if a role emphasizes "Security Operations" as a critical skill and you have relevant experience in this area, you should ensure this keyword prominently features on your resume and LinkedIn profile. Taking this extra step will allow you to stand out over other candidates who don't take the time to tailor their resume or LinkedIn profile toward the role they are applying for.

Next, on the job posting, you will find one of two application methods offered by the company. You may see a blue button with the word "Apply," which, when clicked, redirects you to the company's website to complete their application. The length of these applications will vary depending on the organization. Alternatively, you may encounter the increasingly popular "Easy Apply" feature on a job posting. With this feature, a candidate can apply for the position directly on LinkedIn in seconds. A popup box will prompt you for your email and phone number and to upload your resume. These details can be saved for future applications on LinkedIn, streamlining the process even further. Some companies may ask two or three screening questions to ensure you meet their requirements. Many of these questions only require a simple "yes" or "no" response.

While the "Easy Apply" feature is incredibly efficient, I caution you from utilizing it to submit hundreds of resumes a day for various random roles in many different industries. During Chapter 4, we discussed the importance of tailoring your resume to the job you are applying for. I often find that candidates only utilize one version of their resume for every position they apply for, even if they are entirely unrelated roles. Some feel that sending out dozens or hundreds of applications daily will increase their hiring chances. In reality, you would only be spinning your wheels and potentially damaging your reputation with the companies you apply with.

The next section of the job posting may be one of the most important for you. It is the "Meet the hiring team" section. In this section, you can see the recruiter or hiring manager responsible for the job advertisement. This is a fantastic benefit for you because you will know who will receive your application when you apply. In Chapter 6, we will cover the benefits and methods of reaching out to recruiters and hiring managers when submitting applications.

The last portion of the job posting is the description of the position. These are written by members of the organization and typically include information about the role, including the daily responsibilities and job duties, required and desired qualifications, and other pertinent information. Read the description carefully to ascertain what the organization is looking for and assess if you have the skills needed for the position. While it is ideal to have every qualification the company seeks, I typically advise candidates to consider applying if they feel they meet a minimum of 75% of the requirements.

As we conclude this chapter, I'd like to point out that LinkedIn should not be the only professional networking and job search platform that you utilize in your career transition. Websites such as Indeed, Glassdoor, USAJobs, Dice, ClearanceJobs, and many others are fantastic places to find opportunities in the private sector. Invest time exploring these websites, as some companies utilize specific job boards and not others. I have chosen to focus on LinkedIn in this book as it has been instrumental in my career transition and my successes since. I believe it is the most powerful professional networking platform currently in existence. If you utilize it correctly and to its full potential, it can be an excellent resource as you transition from the Thin Blue Line.

CHAPTER SIX
NAVIGATING THE JOB SEARCH PROCESS

Transitioning from law enforcement to the civilian sector marks a new and exciting time in your professional journey. You have obtained many skills and experiences while on the Thin Blue Line. To successfully switch to the private sector, you need a well-structured and thoughtful approach to the job search process. With a professional-looking resume and a well-crafted LinkedIn profile, you are already on the right track toward securing your dream career in the private sector.

In this chapter, we will delve into the process of identifying exciting opportunities and applying for jobs, how to leverage personal messaging and networking to differentiate yourself from other candidates, and how to be successful in the interview process. I will finish the chapter by giving you a roadmap of your final six months in law enforcement, outlining specific tasks to complete each month to ensure a smooth transition from the Thin Blue Line to the corporate world.

In the previous chapters, we focused on helping you pinpoint industries that align with your interests and qualifications. You have learned the art of showcasing your expertise on your resume and

LinkedIn profile. Additionally, you've started exploring various job boards to gain insight into the different roles available to you in the private sector. It is now time to identify the job opportunities you want to pursue.

Company Research

The civilian job market offers a wide range of opportunities across various industries, each with its own set of challenges and rewards. Finding the correct positions goes beyond just the job title and the salary. Leaving a career in law enforcement is a monumental decision, and it is crucial to ensure you are transitioning to a job, company, and industry that you believe in and where you see long-term career growth opportunities.

I previously warned against applying for dozens or hundreds of jobs a day, as so many candidates try to do. Not only does this make it impossible for you to tailor your resume and application toward each specific role, but it also prevents you from being able to conduct research into the companies to see if they are organizations you even want to be a part of. When you find a position you are interested in, I encourage you to visit the company's LinkedIn page and website. You can learn much about an organization's values, mission, and company culture by what they share on their social media platforms and their website.

A company's website can offer a wealth of information about its products, services, mission, and emphasis on employee well-being. Pay particular attention to the "About Us" or "Our Story" sections to understand the company's history and core values. Visit the "Careers" section to learn about the hiring process, benefits, and other employment-related topics the company chooses to share.

Following a company's social media pages, especially its LinkedIn page, can give you valuable insight into its latest news, updates, job openings, and key priorities. By engaging with the organization's social media platforms, you can also learn about its corporate culture, employee engagement, and relationships. Leverage LinkedIn's networking capabilities to connect with current employees and inquire about their experiences and job satisfaction. Do people seem enthusiastic about their jobs? Can you envision yourself working for such a company? After dedicating years to serving others, you deserve to join an organization that shares your values and will support your career aspirations.

Researching companies by visiting websites like Glassdoor, Indeed, and Comparably can provide valuable insights into the organization. These online platforms provide information about companies, job postings, salaries, and employee reviews. The review section allows current and former employees to anonymously share their opinions about working for a particular company, the company culture, the salaries, and more. Reviewers can also rank their company in various categories, including work-life balance, compensation and benefits, career advancement opportunities, leadership, and overall employee satisfaction.

As you read through the reviews, pay attention to common themes, both positive and negative, as you assess if the organization is one you could see yourself working for. Remember to approach these comments open-mindedly and consider multiple perspectives to get a fair and balanced view of the company. Some individual comments will be overly positive or negative. While you should consider every comment, remember to look at the overall theme of all the reviews. One negative comment amongst dozens of positive ones should not necessarily deter you from applying for a position. However, if you see several concerning comments, you may want to reconsider applying for a role with that company.

I strongly encourage you to utilize all the free information available on companies' websites, their social media platforms, and employee reviews to help you decide. As I mentioned earlier in this book, I failed to recognize employees' overall negative opinions about the company I was joining. I was also negligent in realizing and addressing the company's apparent lack of emphasis on employee well-being and career growth opportunities. I hope you can learn from my mistakes and ensure that you join an organization you can be proud of and one that can help you further your career in the private sector.

Applying to Jobs

Once you have identified companies and positions that interest you, it is time to apply. For some of you, these may be the first applications you have submitted to the private sector. For others, it may have been several years since you have competed in a civilian hiring process. Obtaining a job in the private sector presents a distinct and unique set of challenges compared to the law enforcement hiring process you are accustomed to. In law enforcement, the hiring process predominantly revolves around passing a background check, excelling in the agency's fitness test, undergoing psychological and medical tests, and passing a polygraph examination. While law enforcement departments review your past experiences and qualifications, far less emphasis is placed on your previous educational and professional achievements. Furthermore, the law enforcement hiring process usually adheres to a rigid governmental process, requiring minimal proactive effort on your part. As you will soon discover, the private sector demands a more hands-on approach. It offers different challenges and expectations to complete a hiring process successfully.

One of the first significant differences is the necessity to tailor and adjust your resume for the position you are applying for in the private sector. We already discussed the importance of this step in an earlier chapter; however, it is well worth repeating. Carefully read through the job description, focusing on the skills and experience the company is seeking. If you discover that they are looking for expertise in a particular area in which you have a strong background, it behooves you to add that to your resume. If the company has used different words or phrases to describe skills similar to those on your resume, make minor adjustments to your resume to make it align with the job posting more closely. Instead of applying for dozens of random roles, focus on positions you carefully identified during your research. Then, tailor your resume to fit those specific roles. In the job search process, less is often more.

While tailoring and altering your resume is essential to being a competitive candidate, it is only the first of many. The days of simply applying and waiting to hear back from a company are well behind us. The current job market is fiercely competitive and requires candidates to take additional steps to gain the attention of recruiters and hiring managers. As you have already discovered, LinkedIn provides an excellent overview of an organization and its employees. Many job postings list the recruiter or hiring manager responsible for filling that position. Engaging with these decision-makers on LinkedIn can be a strategic way to stand out from the competition and make a memorable impression during the application process.

I encourage all my candidates to send messages or connection requests to recruiters at the companies they have applied to. When reaching out to a recruiter or hiring manager, it is essential to personalize your message to show your genuine interest in the role and company. Start by introducing yourself and mentioning the specific position you are interested in. Highlight some of the experiences that make you an excellent candidate for the position and express enthusiasm about the role and the company.

Your goal with this message is to gain the recruiter's attention, spark a conversation, and help you stand out over other candidates. Don't simply state your desire to get the job, but focus on showing how your experience and qualifications could be an asset to the organization. Remember, recruiters are incredibly busy, so keep your message concise and to the point. If done correctly, this message can help differentiate yourself from other candidates, build an initial rapport with the recruiter, and increase your chances of progressing to the interview phase of the hiring process.

Here is an example of a message you could send:

Subject: Application for [Job Title] – Eager to Contribute to [Company name]

Dear [recruiter's name],

I hope you are doing well. My name is [your name], and I am writing to express my interest in the [job title] position with your company. As a current [your current position], I have had the opportunity to [briefly mention relevant accomplishments and experience], which I believe has equipped me with the necessary skills and expertise to excel in the [job title] role at [company name]. While reviewing the job posting and your company's LinkedIn page, I was particularly impressed by [specific aspect of the job or company that caught your eye]. My experience, work ethic, and qualifications would make me an asset to your company.

I would love to discuss how my background, skills, and qualifications align with the needs of the [job title] position. If you have any questions regarding my experience or would like to schedule a conversation to discuss my application further, please feel free to contact me at [your phone number] or [your email].

I appreciate your consideration of my application. I look forward to the possibility of contributing to [company name] and am excited about the opportunity to discuss the position with you further.

Sincerely,

[your name]

As you can see, this message is professional and concise, focuses on the candidate's qualifications, and shows an interest in the company and the position. This is a simple yet effective way to connect with important people in the hiring area of your desired companies. Recruiters can advance you to the next rounds or disqualify you from consideration immediately. Going the extra mile of sending a personalized note can significantly elevate your visibility and leave a lasting impression on the recruiter. While some may not respond to your message, many will give you valuable insight into the position, the hiring process, and the company. Remember to be courteous and respectful of the recruiter's time while expressing your enthusiasm for the role.

In addition to engaging directly with recruiters, tap into the professional network you have built to identify and connect with employees at your target company. Leveraging these connections can help you with your job search efforts. LinkedIn allows you to see other platform members who are affiliated with your desired company. You may find that you are already connected with an employee or have a mutual connection with a team member. I encourage you to contact them and inform them of your interest in joining the company. Strike up a conversation, ask questions, and inquire if they can introduce you to anyone involved in the hiring process.

When reaching out to new connections, referencing your mutual acquaintance is an excellent way to break the ice and start the discussion. Companies place significant value and highly prioritize internal referrals during their hiring process. While what you know is undoubtedly important, who you know may be what lands you your dream job. This is one of the many reasons why building a strong professional network is so powerful.

Preparing for the Interview

Your resume, LinkedIn profile, and personal outreach to recruiters get you the interview. However, your performance during the interview is what gets you the job. I have spoken with many candidates who, on paper, appear to be the perfect candidates for the positions I am looking to fill. However, during the interview, they came across as unprofessional, unprepared, and disinterested in the role and the organization. The interview process serves as your chance to showcase your experience and the type of employee you strive to be and to convey your genuine interest in the position and the company. While recruiters primarily assess your hard skills during their initial review of your application, your soft skills exhibited during the interview can set you apart from the other candidates being considered.

The importance of preparing for the interview cannot be overstated. Invest additional time to research the company, its products or services, mission, values, and culture. One question you can expect to be asked is, "Why do you want to work for us?" While this question does not require any technical knowledge, it is one of the most important questions you will be asked. Your answer will demonstrate your effort while preparing for the interview and what you know about the organization. I have spoken with candidates who didn't even know the company name they were interviewing with. This is a sure way to receive the "thanks but no thanks" email, removing you from the hiring process.

When answering why you want to work for the organization, demonstrate your enthusiasm for the position, how you align with the company's values and mission, and why you think you would be an excellent fit. Point to specific examples, including things you saw on their website, articles published about the organization, or social media posts put out by the company. Make it incredibly obvious to the interviewer that you have spent significant time researching and preparing for that interview.

Next, be prepared to answer questions about your background, experience, and qualifications that make you an excellent fit for the position. In the days leading up to the interview, thoroughly review the job description, focusing on the position's duties, responsibilities, and qualifications. Anticipate questions they may ask to gauge your suitability for the position, including matching your skillset and experience with the job requirements. Be ready to provide specific examples of how you tackled similar tasks or challenges in the past. Demonstrate a clear understanding of how your background and expertise align with the responsibilities outlined in the job posting.

A strategy I have found effective when preparing for an interview is to write down the questions you expect to be asked and your responses. Writing down your answers helps solidify them in your memory, allowing you to recall them more efficiently during the interview. Practice verbalizing your answers to a friend or family member to ensure you can articulate your qualifications clearly and confidently.

If you struggle to come up with potential questions, you can also harness the power of Artificial Intelligence (AI) to prepare you for your interviews. Copy and paste the job description into your AI system of choice and ask the AI tool to write ten interview questions based on the job details. You will now have additional questions to consider as you practice and prepare for the upcoming interview.

As you craft responses to potential interview questions, refer back to the list of skills and experiences you documented earlier in this book, focusing particularly on those most closely aligned with the job requirements. Consider how your experience in law enforcement has prepared you to excel in this position with transferable skills such as problem-solving, decision-making, leadership, teamwork, adaptability, and effective communication.

Be ready to provide concrete examples from your law enforcement career where you demonstrated these skills in challenging situations. Focus on instances where you addressed problems, collaborated with a team, managed conflicts effectively, and made impactful contributions to your agency. By highlighting your relevant experience and skills, you will demonstrate your ability to excel in a new position with the company, increasing your chances of being selected for the role. While it may be impossible to predict every question you encounter during an interview, a thorough review of the job description and your qualifications will allow you to approach the interview confidently.

The Interview

With consistent effort and application of the strategies listed in this chapter and throughout this book, you will begin to be asked to interview with companies. Typically, most hiring processes start with a phone screening or video call before progressing to in-person interviews. Some companies conduct two to three rounds of interviews before deciding who will be hired, while others have significantly longer processes. Let's discuss some things to remember and strategies to implement to ensure you successfully highlight your qualifications and suitability for the position.

While this probably seems like common sense to most of you, it always amazes me how many candidates fail to dress appropriately and arrive on time for their interviews. Showing up to a corporate job interview ten minutes late, wearing a t-shirt and jeans, highlights a lack of professionalism and disregard for others' time. Being punctual allows you time to relax, gather your thoughts, and familiarize yourself with the location while displaying your punctuality and reliability. Being well-groomed and well-dressed conveys professionalism, attention to detail, and your serious intent about the position. Remember, you only have one chance to make an excellent first impression.

You probably already submitted your resume when you first applied. However, I encourage you to bring additional copies of your resume and references to the interview. You may be interviewed by someone who wasn't provided with your resume by the recruiting team. Furthermore, many companies tend to ask for a list of references during the interview process. Bringing additional copies of your resume and references showcases your preparedness and attention to detail.

Many behavioral interview questions are typically asked during a private-sector job interview. These questions ask you to provide specific examples from past experiences to demonstrate your skills, abilities, and actions in certain situations. Answering these questions effectively and efficiently requires a plan of action.

One of the best ways to answer behavioral questions is by utilizing the STAR method, which stands for Situation, Task, Action, and Result. This structured approach allows you to provide a comprehensive response while also ensuring that your answer is concise and to the point. When done correctly, the STAR method will enable you to highlight your problem-solving abilities, decision-making skills, and real-world examples of your impact on your organization.

Begin by setting the scene and providing context for the problem you encountered. This is the Situation. Describe the exact issues you were facing, emphasizing the relevance to the question you were asked. Perhaps you can talk about a challenging recruit for whom you were responsible for training and mentoring. You can describe how the trainee failed to follow instructions, continuously forgot critical components of a criminal complaint, or struggled to navigate their way to calls for service. Another potential example of a situation you faced during your time in law enforcement was a long-term speeding issue on a residential road. You can share stories about the complaints you received from citizens and the pressure you were placed under by your sergeant and command staff to solve the issue. Paint a clear picture, allowing the interviewer to grasp the complexities of your challenges.

Next, discuss the Task assigned to you to address the situation. What was expected of you, what were the goals or objectives you were striving to achieve, and what limitations or constraints were you facing? By adequately describing the task, you demonstrate your understanding of your role and responsibilities, highlighting your ability to prioritize assignments and set measurable and achievable outcomes. Using the examples above, perhaps you were instructed by the supervisor of your training division to find a way to connect with your trainee and improve his performance so that he could be released from training on schedule. Or you were tasked with coming up with a long-term solution to address the speeding issues in your assigned sector, thereby reducing the number of severe crashes on a particular roadway or intersection. Share with the interviewer some of the challenges you faced that made the task even more difficult to achieve.

Now that you have shared the situation and the task, it is time to explain the Action you took to address the problem and accomplish the job. Explain the steps you followed, the strategies you employed, and the decisions you made to overcome the various challenges to achieve your goal. Focus mainly on your proactive and creative approach, problem-solving abilities, and the skills you used to navigate the challenge effectively. Be specific by providing examples, demonstrating your initiatives, and your ability to create and follow a plan. Talk about how you brought together several officers and developed training scenarios for your trainee, helping him improve his officer safety skills in a safe and secure environment. Discuss how you deployed sign boards at strategic locations within your sector, advising drivers to drive slower, how you worked with the media relations team to develop a social media campaign to show people the dangers of reckless driving, and the traffic enforcement you conducted to warn or ticket offenders.

Finally, discuss the Result of your actions, emphasizing the positive impact your efforts had on the situation and your agency. Be prepared to highlight any quantitative and qualitative improvements, achievements, or successes directly resulting from your actions. Share how your trainee made remarkable improvements in his performance, lowering the number of corrective actions against him by over 70%, which allowed him to graduate from the field training program on time. This also helped the agency by adding another officer to a patrol shift, lowering the daily average calls for service per officer by three. Highlight how your actions regarding the speeding issue led to an 80% decrease in speeding complaints from the public and a 50% reduction in crashes on that roadway. This resulted in overall citizen satisfaction while reducing the number of crashes dispatched to officers, allowing them to continue patrolling neighbors and deter criminal activity.

Incorporating the STAR method into your interview responses will help you provide a structured and systematic answer to behavioral questions set by the interviewer. It will allow you to highlight critical parts of your experience and achievements while ensuring you stay on topic and provide a brief answer.

Common Interview Questions

While every interview process is unique, and it is impossible to predict every question you may be asked, there are some common ones you can expect to hear throughout your job search process. Here are ten questions I have asked or been asked throughout my career, along with some suggestions on how to format your response.

1. Tell me about yourself.

    This has been the first question I've been asked in nearly every interview process I've ever taken part in and one you will surely get during your transition to the private sector. A mistake I often hear candidates make when answering this question is going off on long-winded tangents about every detail of their life, including where they were born, their dog's name, and their favorite color. Focus on keeping your answer to three to five minutes. Highlight your professional achievements, starting with your current role and working backward from there. Next, articulate your key experiences, skills, and accomplishments, particularly those that best align with the job you are interviewing for. If time permits, consider adding information about your career goals and how they align with the company's mission and values.

2. Why do you want to work for this company?

    This is another very common interview question you can expect to hear. Fortunately, you conducted company research both before you applied and in the days leading up to your interview. Use your answer to this question as an opportunity to show the effort you have put into the process and your knowledge about the company. Talk about their mission and values, the services or products they provide their customers, and specific objectives you would have if given the chance to work for the organization.

3. Describe a challenging situation you faced in your career and how you handled it.

   This is a perfect question to utilize the STAR method to formulate your response! Think of an issue you had at your agency that required an innovative or creative solution. Don't mention how you hated your coworker, so you just stayed away from him. Instead, think about a time when you were given multiple projects at once and had to prioritize, when your agency was implementing a new technology that consistently had issues, or a significant and complex call for service that required you to think and act quickly and decisively. Remember, describe the situation, share the task you were given, explain what actions you took, and then highlight the results of your actions.

4. What are your strengths?

   This is another classic interview question. Use this question to highlight your critical skills and qualifications, particularly those that best align with the job you are applying for. While it may be interesting to share that you are excellent at field sobriety tests, that would probably not be useful when interviewing for a sales specialist position. Instead, focus on your communication skills, work ethic, and ability to connect with strangers. Be sure to give examples from your professional experience to support the areas you describe as your strengths.

5. What are your weaknesses?

   I'm sure you knew this question was coming next. This is a tricky and challenging question to answer as you want to come across as sincere but present yourself positively. However, with proper preparation, you can answer the question honestly while showing some positive qualities. Firstly, be sure to share a real weakness. Avoid cliches such as "I'm a perfectionist" or "I care too much." These are used so often that they come across as insincere. Sharing an actual weakness shows you are self-aware. In addition to providing a weakness and how it has impacted your work in the past, highlight your efforts to overcome it. This shows personal growth and a commitment to further improvement. Finally, explain to the interviewer why your weakness will not hinder your ability to perform the job you are interviewing for and how your strengths are ideal for this position.

6. Why are you leaving your current job?

When answering this question, focus on the future and where you want to go in your career. Describe your career aspirations, your desire to grow, and how this opportunity will give you the challenge and experience needed to make those things happen. Avoid speaking negatively about your current employer; that is an immediate red flag to a recruiter or hiring manager. It is entirely acceptable to note areas that can be improved at your agency; however, do not use this question to vent about your department, your supervisor, or the work itself. Turn this question into a positive by focusing on your long-term goals.

7. Where do you see yourself in five years?

Employers ask this question to understand your long-term career goals and if they align with their organization. Recruiting is a timely and costly effort. Companies don't like constant employee churn, so they prioritize finding candidates they believe will stay and grow with the organization. This is another question where you can highlight the information you have learned about the company. Share how your ambitions align with the company's values and goals. Demonstrate your ambition by emphasizing your desire to grow into more senior and leadership roles and help the company, highlighting a clear vision for your career. Talk about your current skills and the new ones you hope to achieve as you continue to advance, expressing a commitment to the company and the desire to contribute to its success.

8. Can you share an example of when you demonstrated leadership?

This is another excellent question to utilize the STAR method! Companies love asking this question as it allows them to assess your skills and experience, gives them a sense of how you will behave in the future, and to see if you'd be a good fit for the company's culture. Consider a time when you led a long-term project or initiative, took the lead on a very complex call for service that necessitated delegation and other leadership skills, or mentored and coached a younger officer to help him improve his performance on a particular type of call. When answering the question, emphasize your ability to solve problems, make decisions, communicate effectively, and work well in teams. Even if you never held a supervisor position with your agency, that doesn't mean you weren't a leader.

9. How do you handle stress or pressure?

As a current or former law enforcement officer, your answer to this question should be an absolute homerun. Employers want to see that a candidate can handle multiple projects at once, be able to work on tight deadlines, and not get overwhelmed by ever-changing priorities. Fortunately, we have come from a profession where no two days are alike and where we face the possibility of bodily injury or death numerous times throughout our careers. Share examples of stressful situations you encountered while in law enforcement and the strategies and techniques you utilized to deal with them, including prioritization, time management, delegation, and the ability to think clearly during high-stress environments.

10. Do you have any questions for us?

You won't believe how many times I have asked this question to candidates and received nothing but a blank stare in return. When applicants fail to have any questions for the hiring team, it raises some serious red flags in the minds of recruiters and hiring managers. Is the candidate not interested in us? Did he not take the time to prepare questions? How can they have no questions about such a life-altering decision? These things will cross the decision-makers' minds when you fail to ask questions at the end of the interview.

Come prepared with three to five questions to ask your interviewer. Consider questions such as "What are your projected milestones for the person hired for this position in their first six months?" Or "How will you measure the success of the person hired in this position?" One question I always recommend my candidates ask during an interview is, "Do you have any concerns about me as a candidate, and is there any information I can provide to alleviate those concerns?" This is an excellent question as it may allow you to clarify an answer, expand on the part of your experience, or address any other concerns the interviewer may have had about your qualifications.

While interviewing for a new career can be stressful, remember that you have accomplished fantastic things throughout your time in law enforcement and would be an asset to any organization. You have prepared for this moment and are ready to confidently highlight your experience and qualifications. Stand tall, keep excellent eye contact, shake hands firmly, and articulate why you are the best candidate for the role. Finally, thank your interviewers for their time and consideration of your application. Do this as you leave the interview and again via email later in the day. Express your gratitude, make a short statement reconfirming why you feel you are the right candidate for the role, and let them know that you are available for any follow-up questions they may have. This extra step, so often missed by candidates, is absolutely noted and appreciated by recruiters and hiring managers.

 Throughout your job search process, it is important to remain positive and confident in your abilities. Some interviews will go very well, while others may feel shockingly bad. Treat each interview as a learning opportunity and a chance to refine your skills. You may get turned down for a job, even after an interview where you felt you performed exceptionally well. In this extremely competitive job market, minor details can be the deciding factor. Some of these may be completely out of your control. Don't take these rejections personally. Instead, use each experience as an opportunity to learn and grow. With consistent effort and patience, you will soon receive an exhilarating phone call or email letting you know you have landed your dream job!

Salary Negotiations

One of the final steps of the hiring process is salary negotiations. Companies typically list a relatively broad salary range when they post a job advertisement, advising that the salary will be determined "based on the candidate's qualifications." Candidates always hope to be near the upper end, while companies usually plan to offer a salary in the middle or lower end of the range. It's important that you approach salary negotiations with preparation and confidence, not emotion.

Start by researching the industry standards for the role you are offered, considering factors like the location of the position, your experience, and your educational background. Use websites such as Glassdoor, Salary.com, and LinkedIn to see the typical salaries for the position, the industry, and the company, as well as for candidates with similar qualifications. With this information, you can articulate your expectations clearly and support them with concrete data. As uncomfortable as it may seem, remember that salary negotiations are a very normal part of the hiring process, one that employees are expecting.

In addition to salary, consider the complete compensation package, including other benefits such as healthcare, retirement plans, bonuses, and vacation time. While some companies may have limited flexibility on salary, they may be able to offer other perks that can enhance your overall compensation. Consider negotiating a signing bonus, additional days of vacation time, or other types of benefits that are important to you.

Approach these conversations with positivity and flexibility, demonstrating that you are open to finding a mutually beneficial agreement. With proper preparation and effective communication, you can secure a compensation package that reflects your true value. You are now ready to start an amazing new career!

Six-Month Roadmap

To end this chapter, I want to give you a suggested six-month roadmap for your final half a year in law enforcement and what you can do to prepare for a smooth transition. As I am not a financial expert, I will leave the details of your pension and healthcare to those professionals. This roadmap focuses on your career transition into the private sector. Your transition may differ entirely from this schedule, which is fine. Everyone moves at their own pace and prioritizes certain areas over others. You may have years left in your law enforcement career, or your retirement date may be quickly approaching. This roadmap can easily be altered to fit whatever timeline you are on. It has worked very well for many of my clients and myself. I hope it can guide you as you move through this challenging and emotional time of leaving the Thin Blue Line.

Month 6 – Introspection and Goal Setting

If you have not done so, this is an excellent time to reflect on your law enforcement career. Use some of the techniques and practices discussed throughout this book to identify the unique skills you have gained over the years and explore the industries and roles in the private sector that excite you. Take some time to consider what you want your next career to look like. Some of you have spent years in law enforcement, worked long and arduous hours, and seen things that will stay with you forever. Use this month to consider what roles would be fulfilling and help you find purpose in life after law enforcement.

Review job announcements on LinkedIn, USAJobs, ClearanceJobs, and other job boards in your desired industry. Identify reoccurring qualifications or certifications sought by potential employers. Consider the most important ones and start working toward those degrees or certifications. While you may not be able to finish in time for the start of your new career, employers will see your determination and interest in the position and the industry because you have gone the extra mile to pursue further education. Setting a goal will give you something to work toward as you finish your final few months in law enforcement.

Month 5 – LinkedIn Optimization and Strategic Networking

This month revolves around the art of networking. If you couldn't already tell, I am a huge fan of LinkedIn and the power of strategic networking. I am on a mission to encourage every law enforcement officer (any professional, really!) to create a LinkedIn profile and be active on the platform. LinkedIn is a fantastic resource for connecting with decision-makers at companies, learning about certain industries, and connecting with other current and former law enforcement officers.

Ideally, you would have created your LinkedIn profile many years ago and steadily grown your professional network. However, if that is not the case, then there is no better time than the present! Follow the guidelines and suggestions I outlined in Chapter 5 to craft a compelling LinkedIn profile. Remember to include details about your work experience, education, and skills. A properly completed LinkedIn profile can be a game-changer in your job search journey.

If you struggle to grow your network and need assistance, please connect with me on LinkedIn. I'm always excited to add current and former law enforcement officers to my network. Mention reading this book, and I'll gladly accept your connection request and even give you a special mention to my network to help boost your visibility.

This month also presents an excellent opportunity to broaden your network by engaging with professionals in your desired industry, reconnecting with former colleagues, and speaking with others in the private sector. Throughout my career, I have found that people are generally eager to assist others, particularly on a professional platform like LinkedIn. Reach out to recruiters and managers at companies that interest you. Propose a virtual or face-to-face meeting to discover more about their open positions, the company, and the industry. They may offer invaluable insights as you navigate the job application process. You never know what contact may have a drastic impact on your career. Sometimes, who you know is more important than what you know.

Month 4 – Updating Your Resume

This is the month you need to shake the dust off your resume if you haven't already done so. Many law enforcement officers have not considered their resume for many years, sometimes even decades. Some have never written a resume before. Fortunately, you now have the knowledge and tools needed to write a professional-looking resume that will attract the attention of recruiters and hiring managers. With four months to go before leaving the Thin Blue Line, you will want your resume to be polished and as strong as possible to reflect your background and skill set.

Do you need help with your resume? I am proud to offer this service through my company, Recruiting Heroes LLC. We specialize in writing resumes for law enforcement officers, other first responders, and veterans as they prepare to transition to the civilian workforce. Visit the resource section at the back of this book to learn more.

Month 3 – Job Search and Interview Preparation

Your resume and LinkedIn profiles should be polished and ready as you approach the three-month mark. This month, you should spend significant time identifying job opportunities that interest you and submitting applications. With three months to go, you are in a sweet spot. You are not too close to the end to feel extreme pressure to find a job, yet not too far away to cause employers to overlook you as they seek to hire immediately.

Continue searching the various job boards to identify opportunities that catch your eye. Tailor your resume for each job application and start identifying potential employees you can contact within the organization. Reaching out to a member of the company can be a fantastic strategy, allowing you to open doors and give yourself an edge over other applicants.

Over the next couple of months, expect invitations for interviews to begin coming in for the jobs you applied to. View each interview as a valuable opportunity to learn and grow your skills. Prepare for the interview by reviewing the company's website and social media pages, considering the potential questions they may pose, and preparing your answer to those questions. Don't forget to practice utilizing the STAR method when answering behavioral questions. It is an excellent way to answer questions efficiently and comprehensively.

Month 2 – Certifications, Training, and Networking

Remember those certifications and training you identified while reviewing job postings in your desired industry? If you haven't already, you want to start attending classes and taking certification exams this month so you can include them on your resume and mention them during interviews. Research if your desired industry has professional associations or social media groups you can join. These can be fantastic places to ask questions and get suggestions on how to break into the industry. Examine websites such as LinkedIn, Coursera, Udemy, and Skillshare, which offer various online courses and classes. Finally, check your local community college to see what classes they offer that could benefit your future career. Make this month count!

Networking is not a one-and-done activity but an ongoing process. This is particularly true as you transition from law enforcement to the private sector. Industry-specific events can be an excellent way to learn more about your desired industry, make connections, and get your foot in the door with companies. Use online platforms like

Eventbrite and Meetup to find career and networking events in your area. Use these events to engage with professionals in your desired industry. Ask them for any tips they have for breaking into that sector, what their company looks for in candidates they hire, and what you can do to stand out from the crowd. After an event, it is essential to follow up quickly. Connect on LinkedIn, send them a thank you note, and continue the conversation. You want your name to be in their mind as you approach your final weeks before your transition.

Meanwhile, continue exploring job openings in your desired industry. It is time to ramp up your application efforts. Ideally, you should be looking at job opportunities numerous times a week. Make sure to tailor your resume for each job you apply to. This is a time-consuming task, but one that will make a significant difference. Work to identify a recruiter or hiring manager for the role and send them a note on LinkedIn or a personalized email. Thank them for their time and ask if they have a few minutes to talk about their role and the company. Aim to become more than just a name on an application; make a lasting impression.

Month 1 – Final Transition Plans, Goodbyes, and Reflection

Wow, your law enforcement career has come to an end! This final month should be used to reflect on the fantastic career you have had, say goodbye to friends and coworkers, and make final preparations for life after law enforcement. Ensure all human resource paperwork, pensions, and health insurance are handled. If your agency offers exit interviews, I highly recommend you take advantage of it. Failing to do an exit interview is something that I still regret to this day. Don't use the exit interview as a chance to bash your agency. Use it to give constructive feedback that can help current and future officers and the entire agency.

Hopefully, you have received and accepted a job offer as you approach your final days in law enforcement. However, if you haven't landed your next job yet, don't worry! Keep applying for jobs, make connections, attend networking and career events, and follow the steps in this book. Sometimes, it is better to take your time and wait for the right role than to rush into a position that isn't right for you.

I firmly believe that any police officer, deputy sheriff, correctional officer, or federal agent has the potential to do extraordinary things in their careers and lives after law enforcement. During our time on the Thin Blue Line, we experienced so much and gained a wealth of diverse set of skills. This unique background positions us as competitive candidates across an expansive spectrum of industries.

I am always saddened when I speak with a current law enforcement officer who harbors doubts about their ability to succeed outside of the world of policing. Some officers feel confined to security or investigative roles, convinced they would not be qualified for any other position. While a private or corporate security career can be a fantastic choice for some, I urge all law enforcement officers to recognize that it is not their only option. Over the years, I have had the pleasure of speaking with hundreds of former law enforcement officers who have built very successful careers in the private sector. From sales to information technology and even as entrepreneurs, law enforcement officers across America demonstrate the amazing opportunities available to those who have served their communities.

Embrace the notion that you are not bound by the confines of a single industry. I encourage you to pursue opportunities that will bring fulfillment and joy to your life. In the coming chapter, I am honored to share the stories of several former police officers and deputy sheriffs who have left the law enforcement profession and built fantastic careers for themselves in a variety of industries. Know that this is also genuinely possible for you.

CHAPTER SEVEN
FROM SERVICE TO SUCCESS

One of the best parts of my new line of work is hearing from other former law enforcement officers who have successfully transitioned to the private sector and built fantastic careers for themselves. Some have worked their way up the corporate ladder, some have landed themselves remote work opportunities that allow them to spend more time with their families, and others have started their own companies or non-profit organizations. These conversations are a constant reminder of the skills, determination, and grit of those who have served their communities as law enforcement officers.

As you begin to consider your next move after your years of service, it is natural to have feelings of self-doubt and nervousness. You may think that you couldn't possibly succeed in a career outside of law enforcement or that the skills you gained are irrelevant in the civilian world. Nothing could be further from the truth. In this chapter, I am honored to share the success stories of several former police officers and deputy sheriffs who overcame many of these same doubts and have succeeded in building extraordinary lives and careers in the civilian world.

These former officers and deputies have a unique story about their time in uniform, transition, and careers after law enforcement. Some served for over twenty years, while others decided to leave the profession sooner. I am incredibly thankful for their years of service to their communities and for telling their stories. I share these stories with you in hopes that they will inspire you and allow you to approach your transition from law enforcement with the confidence that you can achieve amazing things in the private sector.

Brian Tuskan's Story

Brian Tuskan

Former Police Officer – Honolulu Police Department, Hawaii and Redmond Police Department, Washington

From patrolling the beautiful beaches of Honolulu to assuming the role of Chief Security Officer for a global corporate giant, Brian Tuskan's career trajectory is a testament to the possibilities that await law enforcement officers in their next career. Brian undertook various critical assignments over his 12-year tenure in law enforcement, including SWAT operations, detective work, and narcotics enforcement. His exceptional performance in a complex criminal investigation paved the way for a transition to the private sector, where he continued to excel during his 22-year tenure at Microsoft. His work ethic, depth of knowledge, and steadfast passion culminated in his appointment as Chief Security Officer. Brian remains deeply connected to his law enforcement roots despite his remarkable success in the corporate world. In addition to his corporate responsibilities, he has established a wonderful non-profit organization that serves as a beacon of support for law enforcement officers considering a transition to the private sector. Brian's journey is a powerful reminder of what officers can accomplish in their future careers when they combine their prior experience with the ability to assimilate with their new environment in the corporate world.

Brian began his law enforcement career with the Honolulu Police Department in 1988. His unwavering professionalism and exceptional performance quickly earned him a coveted spot on the agency's full-time SWAT Team, where he played a pivotal role in supporting high-stakes operations, safeguarding heads of state dignitaries, and managing other critical incidents. Brian was also deeply involved as an outreach liaison, working tirelessly to foster stronger ties between the department and the local business community.

After nearly five years with the department, Brian relocated to Washington. He joined the Redmond Police Department, serving in patrol, narcotics, major crimes, and with the Seattle FBI Joint Terrorism Task Force. In 1998, Brian led the investigation of a high-profile burglary at Microsoft, where numerous computers and other devices were stolen. During the months-long investigation, Brian poured over video surveillance footage, data, and other pieces of evidence. He wrote numerous search warrants and conducted dozens of interviews and interrogations, finally unveiling an organized crime operation based in Seattle. The case soon caught the attention of the FBI, and numerous members of the organization were convicted of federal charges.

Brian's fantastic work on this case was also noted by executives at Microsoft, who worked to recruit him to the company for a corporate investigator position. Despite his passion for serving his community as a police officer, Brian knew that the corporate world would open so many opportunities for him that wouldn't be possible in the public sector. Brian accepted the position and left the law enforcement profession in 2000.

Over the next two decades in the private sector, Brian continued to show the same level of expertise and attention to detail as he did in law enforcement. Brian excelled in various positions, from investigations to workplace violence mitigation and executive protection, consistently ascending the corporate ladder. His tenure culminated in his appointment as Microsoft's Chief Security Officer in 2018. Brian held this position until his departure from the company in 2023 to assume the role of Vice President and Chief Security Officer at ServiceNow, a prestigious California-based software development company.

Despite his success in the private sector, Brian has never forgotten his time in law enforcement and remains steadfast in supporting those who wear the badge. Brian founded Cop to Corporate, a non-profit organization that connects law enforcement professionals with a supportive community of allies to aid them in their transition to the private sector and civilian life. Cop to Corporate provides valuable insights and strategies for overcoming challenges typically faced by law enforcement officers looking to start new careers. This excellent non-profit has helped officers worldwide and has amassed an impressive following of thousands of police officers, deputy sheriffs, correctional officers, and federal agents. Check out the resource section at the back of this book for more information on Cop to Corporate and other services that benefit law enforcement officers.

Brian has been an invaluable guide for law enforcement professionals embarking on new careers after years of service. He encourages all those considering a career beyond the Thin Blue Line to build a strong network of fellow officers. Look to those who have transitioned to the private sector, learning from their successes and failures. Utilize resources like Recruiting Heroes and Cop to Corporate to help you through the challenges of finding a new career. Finally, Brian encourages officers to embrace civilian and corporate life fully. While it is important to remember your time as a police officer, deputy sheriff, correctional officer, or federal agent, building new relationships in the private sector is equally important. Learn new ways of looking at situations rather than just through the singular perspective of a law enforcement officer. Be open to change and adapt to a new culture and way of life.

Brian's is a remarkable story about the ability of law enforcement officers to thrive in the corporate world. Allow it to motivate and inspire you to new heights in your next career. Utilize your prior experience and be open to new opportunities, as Brian did throughout his illustrious journey from law enforcement to corporate leadership. You can pursue a rewarding life and a new career after law enforcement by embracing change, cultivating a robust network, and remaining true to your values.

Teresa M. Fitzgerald's Story

Teresa M. Fitzgerald

Former Deputy Sheriff – Livingston County Sheriff's Office, Illinois

Teresa M. Fitzgerald exemplifies the very best qualities of the heroes who serve on the Thin Blue Line. In 2003, Teresa joined the Livingston County Sheriff's Office in Illinois and served as a Patrol Deputy. At the time of her hiring, she was one of only two women working for the entire department. Teresa would not allow the fact that she had entered a heavily male-dominated profession to hold her back. Her work ethic, dedication, passion for her profession, and determination were evident for everyone to see.

Teresa made a name for herself almost immediately upon entering the law enforcement profession. While on a routine traffic stop in 2004, Teresa's investigative skills and her desire to go the extra mile led to her seizing a significant amount of crack cocaine and making the largest narcotics arrest for the entire department that year from a traffic stop. A few months later, Teresa again showed her commitment to serving her community. While patrolling her sector, Teresa came across an overturned vehicle that had been in an accident approximately five minutes earlier. The drunk driver was unconscious in the vehicle, which had caught on fire. Teresa rushed to the man's aid without concern for her own life. She broke out the window, freed the man from the vehicle, and was able to pull him to safety just moments before the entire car became engulfed in flames. Her heroic actions saved the man's life. Teresa was named the Livingston County Sheriff's Deputy of the Year in 2004 for both incidents and her consistent commitment to excellence.

A serious, job-related injury and poor department policy were both leading factors to an early end to Teresa's law enforcement career. At that time, her agency did not offer injured deputies the opportunity to work on light duty, making it challenging for deputies like Teresa to have the time and support they needed to recover from their injuries. While she was determined to return to full duty, she realized that her future was outside law enforcement as she grew her life and aspirations for a family without any light duty policy. Teresa left the Thin Blue Line in 2005 after much contemplation and not finding support in the tough times from her administration. She reflected on that moment and shared that leaving the camaraderie of law enforcement was extremely difficult, perhaps one of the hardest decisions she ever had to make in her life up to that point.

Teresa attributes much of her success in the private sector to her emphasis on networking during her career transition. During the time she was leaving law enforcement, LinkedIn was not yet the powerful platform it is today. Teresa had to rely on emailing, calling, and face-to-face interactions to tell colleagues, friends, and acquaintances about her desire to start a new career. She asked people for their opinions on career paths she should consider, inquired about their profession and the steps she could take to enter that industry, and requested they keep her in mind for current or future opportunities. Her ability to network with professionals in the private sector ultimately led to her discovering her next career. She encourages all law enforcement officers to make networking a significant part of their career transition strategy.

Her tenacity and determination propelled Teresa into the world of finance, where she joined one of the world's largest financial institutions. She began her new career as a New Finance Representative Support Coordinator and worked her way up to various director— and executive-level positions throughout the industry. From a patrol deputy pulling a man from a burning vehicle to a partner-level executive within a Fortune 500 company leading teams in finance, Teresa epitomizes the potential of those who have stood on the Thin Blue Line.

Teresa has never lost the drive and determination she displayed during her years in law enforcement. In 2023, after 17 years of financial advising, planning, and consulting experience across the country with her clients, she founded her own company, Affinity

Planning Partners. She is proud to own a financial planning and consulting firm that helps people all around America with their financial goals proactively and with open communication to better their current financial position. As a fiduciary, Teresa and her team believe in serving their clients with genuine honesty and integrity and focus on listening to what's most important. They help everyday Americans think about their futures by preparing for worst-case scenarios and developing strategies for creating, building, and retaining wealth. Teresa greatly emphasizes determining the most important things to her clients, including their desired lifestyle and the legacy they wish to leave behind for future generations of their families. Teresa continues to support and appreciate the sacrifices our law enforcement officers make every day to protect our freedoms. She is proud to accept current and former law enforcement officers and first responders as clients and offers them a discount for her services. She's also happy to pay it forward and help anyone network anytime.

Teresa has several pieces of advice for those leaving the Thin Blue Line, including the importance of networking, finding a mentor, believing in your dream regardless of age, and enjoying life outside of the badge. As discussed extensively throughout this book, your ability to network will majorly impact your chances of finding an excellent career outside of law enforcement. A mentor will be particularly important in the first months and years of your new career. They can share their experience and give advice for excelling in your new industry. Lean on the expertise and guidance of others, and never be afraid of pursuing new challenges. Whether you are 30 or 60, when you leave law enforcement, it is never too late to start a new career and identify new passions. Finally, enjoy your life and embrace the freedom that life outside of law enforcement can bring. While the urge to serve and to put others first will always be an integral part of who we are as former law enforcement officers, it is okay to think about yourself and allow a new generation of heroes to hold the Thin Blue Line.

Steven Meincke's Story

Steven Meincke

Former Lieutenant – Arlington County Police Department, Virginia

From a nearly three-decade law enforcement career to the Senior Corporate Security Manager for one of the world's largest food and beverage companies, Steven Meincke's journey on and beyond the Thin Blue Line should inspire any law enforcement officer. Steve started his career as a police officer for the United States Capital Police before joining the Arlington County Police Department, dedicating over 28 years to safeguarding communities in and around our nation's capital. With three years at the Capital and 25 at Arlington, his commitment to the law enforcement profession is evident, and he continues to support his brothers and sisters in blue by mentoring and advising officers considering their subsequent careers.

Throughout his illustrious law enforcement journey, Steve's unwavering dedication saw him obtain numerous diverse roles in Patrol, Motors, Special Operations Section, and more. Rising through the ranks from Police Officer to Lieutenant, his career highlights his excellent performance and sense of duty. Like many law enforcement officers, Steve and his family made numerous sacrifices to allow him to succeed in his career. He worked long hours and many overnight shifts, often missing birthdays, holidays, and other special occasions. Steve acknowledges that he has a deep appreciation and gratitude for his wife, who always supported his ambitions and often had to serve as a single parent while raising their children.

Steve confessed that, even after 28 years of service, he did not intend to leave law enforcement. However, he was soon presented with an opportunity that was too good to ignore when Nestlé, an internationally recognized brand, relocated its American headquarters to Arlington, Virginia. A friend within the company informed Steve of a senior position in the corporation's security team.

Initially hesitant to depart from the law enforcement profession, Steve nevertheless agreed to be considered for the position and went through the interview process. His knowledge and expertise in security and investigations were immediately recognized by the leadership team of Nestlé, who offered him the position of Senior Corporate Security Manager. The position came with a fantastic salary, substantial benefits, and the opportunity for Steve to have new experiences in the private sector. Steve accepted the job offer and left the law enforcement profession in May 2019.

Steve admitted that the first six months outside of law enforcement were challenging. He had left a profession that had become a significant part of his life and identity. Despite his excitement to experience something new, he missed his colleagues and law enforcement friends. He had entered an entirely new industry with different processes, procedures, and cultures. Fortunately, Steve was able to build a strong relationship with his supervisor, who became a guiding mentor for him. This relationship was instrumental in Steve's smooth transition to the private sector, and he believes every law enforcement officer should strive to find a mentor who can guide them through the process of leaving law enforcement and starting a new career.

In addition to his work at Nestlé, Steve enjoys helping and supporting other law enforcement officers as they prepare for their next careers. He often speaks with current officers about the importance of networking and having a strong resume. Steve believes his connection with an employee at his current company was a major factor in his being offered the position. He understands just how competitive the job market can be and acknowledges that he may not have even been invited to interview for the role had he simply applied for the job instead of being referred. Furthermore, Steve has found that many law enforcement officers fail to write effective resumes for the private sector. He believes officers must articulate their qualifications, highlight their achievements, and demonstrate how the skills learned during a law enforcement career can translate to positions in the civilian workforce.

With nearly three decades of law enforcement service behind him, Steve continues to exemplify the traits and characteristics we hope to see in our police officers, deputy sheriffs, and other members of the Thin Blue Line. Steve's story underscores the incredible potential of our law enforcement officers as they enter the private sector. He remains connected to his brothers and sisters in uniform by his determination to share his experiences and advise others looking to transition to a civilian career and life. Steve believes wholeheartedly that the skills forged during a career in public service are invaluable assets for companies of all industries. Let Steve's success story inspire and motivate you as you look to your future after your years in the uniform.

Matthew Mancini's Story

Matthew Mancini

Former Deputy Sheriff – Loudoun County Sheriff's Office, Virginia

Entering the Loudoun County Sheriff's Office fresh out of college, Matt, an eager 22-year-old, embarked on a lifelong dream to pursue a career in law enforcement. Back in 2013, when Matt entered the profession, there was an abundance of candidates looking to become law enforcement officers. Matt was one of over 100 candidates to attend the agency's Physical Ability Assessment, with only a handful of open positions available. He still remembers his pride and excitement upon finding out he was being hired as a patrol deputy for Virginia's largest, full-service sheriff's office.

Matt thoroughly enjoyed his ten years in law enforcement, during which he had the opportunity to work on patrol, as a school resource officer, and finally, as a background investigator for the agency's employment services section. Success seemed to follow Matt throughout much of his career. During his time in the unit, the School Resource Officer program received national recognition when the Loudoun County Sheriff's Office was named the Model

Agency of the Year by the National Association of School Resource Officers. Several years later, Matt was heavily involved in the recruiting and hiring effort, leading the agency to its lowest vacancy rate in decades.

Despite his passion and pride in his work, Matt began contemplating moving away from law enforcement. He had served his community for over a decade and had experienced many of life's milestones during that time, including getting married, buying his first home, and having children. Being a deputy sheriff was the only career he had ever known, yet he felt the urge to experience life outside the uniform.

Matt has always valued being there for his family. The long hours, mandatory overtime, and salary were major factors that led him to consider leaving the profession at this career stage. He weighed the pros and cons of entering the private sector, ensuring he was not making a rushed decision. It soon became clear to him that he was ready for a new challenge and the chance to be there to watch his kids grow up.

During his career transition, Matt experienced many of the same hardships so often faced by law enforcement officers looking to enter the private sector. He received several rejections and was outright ignored by multiple companies. Matt was also offered positions with companies that did not align with his career aspirations. Fortunately, he was determined to find a career that inspired him and vowed not to leave law enforcement for anything less. This should be a powerful reminder for any officer contemplating leaving the Thin Blue Line. While the urge to find your next career may seem overwhelming, don't allow frustration or impatience to drive you into a hasty decision. Take the time to ensure that your transition out of law enforcement is done thoughtfully and that you wait for the right opportunity that aligns with your interests, aspirations, and values.

Matt's job search process is another fantastic example of the power of a strong network. Despite several frustrating experiences applying and interviewing with companies in the private sector, Matt remained positive and spoke to friends, neighbors, and colleagues about his career aspirations. One of these conversations was with a high-ranking executive for a large government contractor. She was immediately impressed with Matt's background, determination, and investigative experience. She informed him about a fully remote Management Analyst position that had just become available with her company and encouraged him to apply, which Matt did. He was almost immediately invited to participate in the interview process and was soon offered the position. While Matt's skills and personality were undoubtedly a major factor, his ability to network with a decision-maker at the company helped secure him this excellent role.

Matt has discovered joy and excitement in his new career six months since leaving law enforcement. Despite entering an entirely different industry, he has hit the ground running and has achieved immediate success. Matt has had the opportunity to work on significant projects and interact with influential federal government members. Matt attributes his smooth transition out of law enforcement to his ability to adapt and encourages other officers to embrace change when entering the private sector. It is entirely natural to feel uncertain when starting a new career; however, being open to new experiences and ways of doing things is crucial to your long-term success. Being resistant to change and stuck in old mindsets can seriously hinder your ability to adjust to life in the civilian workforce.

Matt continues to look back fondly on his time in law enforcement and is passionate about helping other officers make successful transitions to the private sector. In addition to his full-time job, he has joined my team at Recruiting Heroes as a part-time recruiter, working to find amazing careers for America's law enforcement officers and veterans. Having spent nearly a third of his life in uniform, Matt will never forget the service and sacrifices made by our heroes in law enforcement.

These are just a few of the incredible stories of officers who left their careers at various points and went on to achieve great success in the private sector. Whether you are considering a career change after only a few years in uniform, like Teresa, or after decades of service, like Steven, there are numerous stories of officers like you who took the necessary steps to find fulfillment after leaving law enforcement.

As you consider your own transition, let these stories serve as a source of motivation and inspiration during moments of doubt or uncertainty. Leaving a career like law enforcement can be extremely daunting, and many officers struggle with confidence and belief in their abilities. Realize that countless officers have been in your exact situation and have successfully navigated these challenges. Let their stories be a constant reminder of your potential as you strive to achieve new heights in your next career.

CHAPTER EIGHT
LIFE BEYOND THE
THIN BLUE LINE

The memory of my last day in law enforcement remains vivid in my mind, a bittersweet day of mixed emotions. I will never forget the feeling of walking out the door of my agency after my final shift, knowing that my career as a deputy sheriff was over. A bright and exciting future lay ahead of me, but the passion to serve and the bonds of friendship I had formed weighed heavily on my mind. I was about to enter a completely new and different world from what I was accustomed to. I would no longer be working to protect my community but rather to advance a company's mission. Amidst the anticipation and excitement for my future, I felt a sense of guilt for leaving behind friends and colleagues who continue to brave the dangers of their profession. However, despite my mixed emotions, there was also a certainty in my decision. Though my road ahead was entirely new to me, I was prepared to face life beyond the Thin Blue Line.

During the first few days, weeks, and months of your transition to the private sector, you will undoubtedly feel similar emotions. Many former officers express an initial loss of purpose and uncertainty about the future when they first leave the law enforcement profession. You have spent years, perhaps even decades, with well-defined expectations and objectives. Keeping the community and the country safe was your mission. Losing that purpose can be extremely challenging for some officers, deputies, and agents to handle. I encourage you to accept that these are very normal and appropriate feelings to have after leaving such an identity-defining career. However, remember that this journey is about self-discovery and reinvention. Embrace the possibilities that lie ahead as you embark on a new chapter beyond law enforcement.

Tackle the challenges and seize the opportunities that come with starting a new career, and don't let doubt and uncertainty hold you back from your true potential. It is very common for former officers to grapple with imposter syndrome when they start a new position, particularly if it is in an industry far removed from law enforcement, security, or investigations. Imposter syndrome manifests as a constant feeling of self-doubt and inadequacy, where people believe they are not enough and fear they will be exposed as frauds. Despite mounting evidence to the contrary, some former law enforcement officers believe they cannot succeed in the private sector and do not have the necessary skills to be an asset to their new company. They believe that the skills and qualifications required to succeed in their new role are miles apart from what they are accustomed to in the world of policing.

During these moments of doubt, reflect on your list of accomplishments and the transferable skills you have honed throughout your career. By recalling your achievements and qualifications, you can combat feelings of inadequacy and uncertainty. They will allow you to approach your new career with a sense of excitement and confidence. The skills you have gained are not bound by the confines of a specific industry but are translatable tools you can apply to any sector of the job market. By embracing this perspective, you can leverage your strengths and experience to transform perceived challenges into opportunities for growth and development.

While you will obviously have much to learn, your prior experiences will be a valuable asset to your new company. Colleagues will seek your advice and value your unique perspective on various topics. Be confident in your responses and utilize the knowledge gained during a diverse law enforcement career to address new challenges in the private sector. As I emphasized extensively throughout this book, you will be pleasantly surprised by how seamlessly many of your skills and experiences will translate into your new role, enabling you to make an immediate impact on your organization.

However, being receptive and open-minded to new ideas and approaches in your new work environment is also important. Learning and adapting to a culture and organizational processes may be a significant challenge for former law enforcement officers, who are accustomed to the formal and structured nature of policing. I had an initial moment of culture shock within the first few weeks in my new role. Coming from an agency with a relatively strict policy of following the chain of command, I was initially taken aback by the lack of oversight at my new organization. Employees were expected to make their own decisions and independently develop and implement new ideas without seeking approval from higher-ranking members of the company. Be prepared to encounter an entirely different environment in your new position from what you are accustomed to in law enforcement. Fortunately, prior officers have inherent skills of adaptability that they have gained during the unpredictable nature of law enforcement. Trust in your abilities and seize the opportunity in your new career.

Finding a mentor during the early stages of your career can be an effective way of getting up to speed in a new industry. Whether your mentor is an experienced member of your company, a former police officer with several years of experience in the private sector, or a seasoned professional with a long history of success in your industry, mentors can provide valuable insights, advice, and strategies as you get settled in your position. By tapping into the wisdom and experience of others, you can learn from their successes and failures. Their wealth of knowledge will allow you to quickly adjust to your new environment and maximize opportunities in your new career.

I was fortunate to have had a very supportive supervisor in my first role outside of law enforcement. Richard soon became both a mentor and a friend. Though he held a much more senior role in the organization, Richard had spent many years as a recruiter and knew the challenges associated with this role. While he was never in law enforcement, Richard understood this was an entirely new environment for me. He took me under his wing and was a continuous resource as I navigated through the first few months in the private sector.

I encourage you to find a mentor to celebrate your successes and discuss your frustrations. Having someone by your side who can share their expertise and listen to your challenges can be monumental in ensuring a smooth transition to the private sector. As someone who has dedicated his post-law enforcement life to helping my brothers and sisters in blue, I am always available to help where I can. I encourage you to contact me via LinkedIn or my author website, www. WhittingtonBooks.com.

Beyond just your new job, transitioning from the Thin Blue Line can open a world of new opportunities and experiences for you. Embrace this newfound freedom to identify interests and hobbies that may have taken a backseat during your time in law enforcement. Are there dreams that were put on hold during your days as an officer? Perhaps you want to open a business, write a book, get an advanced degree, or start a podcast. Believe me when I tell you, the sky is the limit for those who come from a life of service.

Personally, the freedom and flexibility of a job in the corporate world allowed me to discover a new venture I had never previously considered. Just two months after leaving the sheriff's office, I founded Recruiting Heroes LLC, an employment agency dedicated to finding amazing careers for America's veterans and first responders following their years of service. I started this company as a side hustle due to the number of messages I received from veterans and law enforcement officers around America asking for help and advice on transitioning to the private sector.

As I had never taken so much as a single business class in my entire life, I didn't expect my company to ever evolve into anything more than just a hobby. However, within a few months, Recruiting Heroes exploded into an incredibly successful company, allowing me to leave the world of employment and experience the thrill of entrepreneurship. Recruiting Heroes now works with dozens of international and American corporations and has helped hundreds of veterans and first responders find their subsequent careers.

You should use this time in your career to pursue your passions and watch them transform your life. The path of continuous development should not stop when you enter the private sector. This is simply the next step in your ongoing journey. Take this moment to develop a long-term plan for your life, considering where you want to be in the years ahead. Identify tangible goals you want to achieve in all facets of your life, be it advancing your career, exploring entrepreneurial opportunities, or any other major areas. Don't look back on your life with regret. One of my all-time favorite speakers, the late Jim Rohn, once said, "The worst thing one can do is not to try, to be aware of what one wants and not give in to it, to spend years in silent hurt wondering if something could have materialized – never knowing."

In recent years, I have made a deliberate effort to take on challenges that excite and frighten me in pursuing my dreams. Some of these things include competing in an Ironman triathlon, starting my own business, leaving my full-time job to run my business, and now writing this book. These have all been leaps of faith that initially terrified me but have now become some of the best decisions of my life. I encourage you to use this time to explore and follow your dreams and aspirations. Once again, believe me when I tell you the sky is the limit for those who have worn the uniform and protected their country.

Life beyond the Thin Blue Line meant that I could also finally spend significantly more time with my wife and family, a luxury that was previously difficult to enjoy due to the demands of my profession. Gone were the days of missed birthdays, holidays, and other special occasions. During my early years in law enforcement, I would voluntarily work on major holidays, allowing deputies with children to be home to celebrate with their families. Throughout my law enforcement career, I was also accustomed to being constantly glued to my work phone in fear of missing a significant message or call from a superior. The transition to the private sector brought a profound sense of relief as I could finally embrace the feeling of being completely off the clock. This newfound peace of mind allowed me to be entirely present during important moments with my family.

The sacrifices made by the families of law enforcement officers cannot be overstated. Their unwavering support allowed us to pursue a life of service, often spending significantly more time with strangers than with our loved ones. As you embark on a new journey in the private sector, remember your family's commitment and sacrifices by prioritizing quality time with them. Make up for moments missed during your days in uniform, seizing every opportunity to make lasting memories with your wife, children, and extended families. Don't allow the hustle and bustle of corporate life to distract you from the importance of family, for they have been the foundation of our strength during our years of service.

Finally, remember to take care of yourself physically and mentally. As law enforcement officers, we put our bodies and minds through constant stress and turmoil. An average citizen experiences traumatic incidents only a few times throughout their entire lives. On the other hand, an average police officer responds to these types of events nearly daily. We interact with some of the worst members of society and see many horrific things. We work long hours, are likely to be involved in physical altercations, and often run on fast food and caffeine. This type of lifestyle will take a toll on almost anyone. Many law enforcement officers become overweight, and we have a significantly higher likelihood of dying by suicide than the average American.

Whether from the things I saw, the stress, or some other factor, I experienced night terrors and sleepwalking episodes throughout much of my law enforcement career. My wife would wake to me running from the room, attempting to open doors, or yelling about someone being in our house. These episodes terrified her and left me covered in sweat, with my heart pounding. While I still have the occasional episode, they have significantly decreased since leaving law enforcement. I hope your new chapter in life will bring similar peace and calmness following a career of stress and constant pressure. Make a concrete effort to prioritize your health and well-being as you transition to civilian life.

As you approach the end of your time in law enforcement, remember that this is not the end but a new beginning. Each step throughout your law enforcement journey has prepared you for this moment. You are equipped with the skills, knowledge, and resilience to thrive in any industry and become an outstanding member of your new organization. Remember that a successful transition takes time and patience. Some of you may find your next calling on the first try, while others may require experimentation and trial and error before finding your dream career.

The strategies we have discussed throughout this book can continue serving you throughout your career in the private sector. You should constantly review your transferable skills, improve your resume and LinkedIn profile, and expand your professional network. These key areas can help transform your career far beyond your expectations. Strive for continuous growth, identify new opportunities, and continue displaying the passion and work ethic from your time in law enforcement.

As I wrote this book, I was able to reflect on my time in law enforcement and remember some of the incredible moments I experienced. I will always be thankful to the Loudoun County Sheriff's Office, the leadership team, and my friends and colleagues who I served alongside. My time in law enforcement has changed me forever. I see the world through a different lens and appreciate the immense service and sacrifices required to allow me to live the American Dream. Though I faced many of the typical hardships experienced by our men and women in uniform, I know I would not be where I am today without those wonderful years as a deputy sheriff. I am eternally grateful. I have stood on the Thin Blue Line.

CANDIDATE RESOURCES

Throughout this book, I mentioned several resources, websites, and certifications that can help you in your career transition and bring you success in the private sector. While there are undoubtedly others, these are ones that I have personal experience with or have received numerous positive reviews from trusted sources.

Recruiting Heroes LLC—I am the proud founder and CEO of Recruiting Heroes LLC. We are dedicated to finding amazing careers for America's law enforcement officers and veterans. Our candidate services include resume writing, LinkedIn profile optimization, interviewing training, and reverse recruiting. We also work with companies around America that need help finding talented people to join their teams. Learn more about us by visiting our website, www.RecruitingHeroesLLC.com, or LinkedIn page.

Cop To Corporate – Cop to Corporate is a fantastic non-profit organization that has been helping law enforcement officers transition to the private sector for over a decade. Brian Tuskan, a former police officer and founder of Cop to Corporate, provides excellent resources to help officers prepare for life in the private sector. www.coptocorporate.com

Job Search Platform

LinkedIn: www.LinkedIn.com

Dice: www.Dice.com

USAJobs: www.USAJobs.gov

ClearanceJobs: www.ClearanceJobs.com

Indeed: www.Indeed.com

Employee Review Websites:

Glassdoor: www.glassdoor.com

Indeed: www.Indeed.com

Comparably: www.comparably.com

Resume and LinkedIn Resources:

Free resume templates are available in various places, including www.resume.com, www.canva.com, and Microsoft Word. You can also download my all-time favorite resume template on my author's website, www.WhittingtonBooks.com. My website also has a free guide on optimizing your LinkedIn profile.

Do you want me to write a professional resume or optimize your LinkedIn profile? Visit my company's page to book a consultation with me. Mention reading this book and get 25% off any of our services! Post a picture of yourself reading this book and receive 50% off any of our services! www.RecruitingHeroesLLC.com.

Finding Networking Events

Eventbrite: www.Eventbrite.com

Meetup: www.Meetup.com

Certifications

Cybersecurity

CompTIA: www.CompTIA.org

Certified Information Security Manager (CISM): www.cismcourse.com

Private Security

Certified Protection Professional (CPP) from ASIS International: www.asisonline.org

Certified Security Consultant (CSC) from the International Association of Professional Security Consultants (IAPSC): www.iapsc.org

Corporate Security & Risk Management

Certified Fraud Examiner (CFE) from the Association of Certified Fraud Examiners: www.acfe.com

Project Management Professional (PMP) from the Project Management Institute (PMI): www.pmi.org

Emergency Management

Certified Emergency Manager (CEM) from the International Association of Emergency Managers (IAEM): www.iaem.org

Certified Business Continuity Professional (CBCP) from the Disaster Recovery Institute International (DRI) www.drii.org

Investigations & Forensics

Certified Forensic Interviewer (CFI) from the Center for Interviewer Standards and Assessments: www.certifiedinterviwer.com

Certified Computer Examiner (CCE) from the International Society of Forensic Computer Examiners (ISFCE): www.isfce.com

Human Resources & Organizational Development

Senior Professional in Human Resources (SPHR): www.shrm.org

Certified Professional in Learning and Performance (CPLP) from the Association for Talent Development (ATD): www.td.org

Training & Education

Certified Training and Development Professional (CTDP) from the Institute for Performance and Learning: www.performance-andlearning.ca

Certified Professional in Learning and Performance (CPLP) from the Association for Talent Development (ATD): www.td.org

Certified Online Training Professional (COTP) from the International Council for Certified Online Training Professionals (ICCOTP): www.iccotp.com

Project Management

Project Management Professional (PMP) from the Project Management Institute (PMI): www.pmi.org

PRINCE2 Practitioner from AXELOS: www.axelos.com

Legal & Compliance

Certified Compliance & Ethics Professional (CCEP) from the Society of Corporate Compliance and Ethics (SCCE): www.corporatecompliance.org

Certified Anti-Money Laundering Specialist (CAMS) from the Association of Certified Anti-Money Laundering Specialists (ACAMS): www.acams.org

Certified Regulatory Compliance Manager (CRCM) from the American Bankers Association (ABA): www.aba.com

ACKNOWLEDGMENTS

This book would never have been possible without my fellow law enforcement officers who supported me throughout my career. My close friends Jeremy Krapfl, Eric Urbain, and Mitch Costic were with me on many of my toughest calls for service and always had my six. I thank Sheriff Mike Chapman and the leadership team of the Loudoun County Sheriff's Office for their faith in me and for allowing me to have such an incredible career.

I'd also like to thank my wife, Shelby, for always believing in me and for all her hard work editing *Beyond the Thin Blue Line*. Her amazing skills as an English teacher were instrumental in helping this former law enforcement officer with no writing background complete his first book. To my family, Michael Whittington, Kathy Whittington, Brendan Whittington, Brittany Whittington, Roy Hall, Nancy Hall, and Derek Hall, you mean more to me than I can put into words. I am truly blessed to have such a loving and supportive family.

I am incredibly thankful to Teresa Fitzgerald, Brian Tuskan, Steven Meincke, and Matthew Mancini for sharing their amazing stories with me. You are an inspiration to law enforcement officers around the country.

To my incredible Book Launch Squad, your efforts in promoting *Beyond the Thin Blue Line* mean the absolute world to me. This book could never have reached its heights without your hard work and passion. Thank you, Michael Zimmerman, Stephen Lockard, Chris Roertgen, Steven Meincke, Tim Ortwein, Tom Slaten, Jody Donaldson, Christine Curtis, Joshua Malczak, Angel Bolton, Claudia McMicken, Justine Amado, Jeffrey Miller, Alma Burke, Marialyce Winreich, Eric Urbain, Brad Johnson, Justin Nyce, Teresa Fitzgerald, Matthew Mancini, Dianna Brady, Colby Pickering, Tracy Paugh, and Alexandra Wilson.

Thank you all!

Colin

SERVICE TO SUCCESS

While writing *Beyond the Thin Blue Line*, I had the opportunity and honor of speaking with dozens of law enforcement officers, other first responders, and military veterans. These heroes had unique stories about serving their communities and their country. Some shared horrifying accounts of surviving an active violence incident or talked about their experience in Iraq and Afghanistan. Others told heartwarming stories of lives they saved and people they helped. The American spirit, passion, and bravery were evident in every story I heard.

All these men and women deserve to have their stories told. They have inspired me to write my next book. Service to success will share true stories of American heroes who have served in the United States Armed Forces or as a first responder. I will celebrate their success and reflect on their challenges. Feats of heroism, mental health, career transitions, and life after service will be prevailing topics throughout this book.

Visit www.WhittingtonBooks.com to follow my progress on this book or to share your story.

COLIN WHITTINGTON

ABOUT THE AUTHOR

Colin Whittington is a former deputy sheriff, founder, and Chief Executive Officer of Recruiting Heroes LLC. Colin started his law enforcement career as a patrol deputy for the Loudoun County Sheriff's Office, Virginia's largest, full-service sheriff's office. Within his first two years, he received two Life Saving Awards for two separate incidents. In 2019, the Virginia Sheriff's Association named Colin the Virginia Deputy Sheriff of the Year. Colin was then promoted to Sergeant and was charged with running the recruiting, background investigation, and hiring unit for the Loudoun County Sheriff's Office. He supervised a team of recruiters and background investigators. While law enforcement agencies around the nation struggled to attract talent, Colin's team led the agency to a record-low vacancy rate through innovative and strategic recruiting strategies.

Colin left law enforcement in 2022 and became the recruiting director for an information technology firm in northern Virginia, where he recruited top talent for positions with the federal government and major corporations. Colin never forgot his brothers and sisters on the Thin Blue Line during this time. He received countless messages from police officers, deputy sheriffs, and federal agents from around America seeking advice and help on how they could successfully transition to the private sector.

The lack of resources available to our law enforcement officers inspired Colin to start his own business. Recruiting Heroes LLC is an employment agency dedicated to finding amazing careers for America's veterans and first responders. Colin and his team work with companies and candidates around the country. He offers resume writing, LinkedIn profile optimization, and interview training for officers looking to find new careers after their years of service. Recruiting Heroes helps companies looking to bring fantastic candidates to their teams, particularly those looking to hire veterans and first responders.

Colin enjoys spending time with his family, playing soccer, and competing in Ironman triathlons in his free time.

www.WhittingtonBooks.com

Colin.Whittington@RecruitingHeroesLLC.com

COLIN WHITTINGTON

www.ingramcontent.com/pod-product-compliance
Lightning Source LLC
Chambersburg PA
CBHW070722130626
46553CB00005B/2101